Counselling
People on
Prescribed
Drugs

Counselling in Practice

Series editor: Windy Dryden
Associate editor: E. Thomas Dowd

Counselling in Practice is a series of books developed especially for counsellors and students of counselling which provides practical, accessible guidelines for dealing with clients with specific, but very common, problems.

Counselling People on Prescribed Drugs

Diane Hammersley

SAGE Publications
London • Thousand Oaks • New Delhi

First published 1995

SAGE Publications Ltd
6 Bonhill Street
London EC2A 4PU

SAGE Publications Inc
2455 Teller Road
Thousand Oaks, California 91320

SAGE Publications India Pvt Ltd
32, M-Block Market
Greater Kailash – I
New Delhi 110 048

British Library Cataloguing in Publication data

A catalogue record for this book is available from the British
Library.

ISBN 0 8039 8886 9
ISBN 0 8039 8887 7 (pbk)

Library of Congress catalog card number 95-067893

Typeset by Mayhew Typesetting, Rhayader, Powys
Printed in Great Britain by Biddles Ltd, Guildford, Surrey

Contents

Preface

This book has its origins in The Withdraw Project started by Moira Hamlin in 1985 and which I joined in 1986. The Project offered a psychological treatment for people who wanted to withdraw from benzodiazepines, with a three-year research study running alongside it, and was in contact with several hundred clients, doctors and other professionals. As the research group was followed up, the work expanded to include other drugs, the psychological effects of drugs and how to adapt therapy to working with these clients. I am grateful for their time and patience in allowing me to learn from them.

Moira and I went on to set up workshops to disseminate the findings and to train drug workers and counsellors in how to withdraw benzodiazepines while teaching people alternatives. Many people who came to workshops raised their clinical difficulties, shared with us the problems and solutions they had found, and in many ways contributed to some of the questions addressed here.

As we discovered the implications of counsellors not taking drugs into account in their work, we realized that these findings had wider relevance. All counsellors and psychotherapists, not just specialist drug workers, needed to be aware of the part that drugs might be playing in their clients' lives. Much counselling is rendered ineffective; many clients remain frustrated at lack of progress; much 'stuckness' remains unexplained.

In writing a book which starts from the basics, I recognize that I have treated many topics superficially and described complex processes simplistically. There are other books which deal with clients' problems in greater depth and pharmacological mechanisms with more precision which I hope readers will go on to explore. I have only briefly touched on counselling clients with more serious mental illnesses or psychological problems which experienced practitioners will be working with, but which are beyond the scope of this book.

I want to acknowledge my indebtedness to Moira Hamlin who as director of The Withdraw Project set me off on this path. As a colleague it has become increasingly difficult to know who contributed what, but she has been a major influence on my thinking. I am particularly grateful for her encouragement to think creatively about my clinical experience, test new ideas and take risks to challenge sacred cows and develop new ways of working. Finally, my thanks go to Windy Dryden for his wise advice about the overall shape and feel of the book.

Diane Hammersley

1

The Purpose of Prescribing

For historical and sociological reasons doctors in the past have treated psychological problems within a medical frame of reference and without involving other professions in the early stages of treatment. Counsellors from other professions have a different perspective and need to understand the medical one if their client is being treated medically. The assumption that prescribing can be left entirely to the doctor is not valid and can lead to harmful consequences, as well as seriously undermining counselling.

The 1980s saw a growing awareness of the problems of prescribed drugs and the difficulties faced by people dependent on benzodiazepines (tranquillizers and sleeping tablets). Psychologists and drug workers were busy developing and investigating safe, effective ways to withdraw these drugs and a strong self-help movement got under way with a campaigning brief which led to legal action against pharmaceutical companies and some doctors.

While the search was on for better non-addictive alternatives, and pharmaceutical companies vied with each other to produce a 'wonder drug' with no side-effects, patients and their counsellors began to question the wisdom of relying on drugs at all since drugs do not treat the underlying problem. Developments in medical training and a growing sympathy and respect for complementary therapies among some doctors led to a greater willingness to consider counselling not just as a viable alternative but as the treatment of choice.

It was widely accepted by both counsellors and doctors that medication primarily for people who were ill, and counselling for the 'worried well', were entirely compatible. Either approach could be added to the other and would probably increase the effectiveness of both. However the issue is not so clear cut and medication and counselling cannot be viewed as separate approaches which combine comfortably. Drugs affect people psychologically and therefore affect counselling in ways that are sometimes helpful and sometimes not.

Whenever a person taking psychotropic drugs seeks counselling, he has already accepted help from someone else, and implicitly acknowledged that his problem can be seen and treated as a medical one. He may recognize that his problem is fundamentally a psychological one but believe that emotional problems may be helped in some way by drugs even if only for the relief of symptoms. Alternatively he may believe that drugs are his treatment and counselling merely an adjunct of it.

Two recent developments have added to the climate for changing the established ways of thinking. First, there has been a movement in health care towards increasing individual rights and responsibilities in terms of access to information, being offered alternatives and the patient's right to choose. Secondly, the development of multi-disciplinary working requires a wider understanding of the range of therapeutic approaches both in theory and practice among those who work cooperatively. The hierarchy that puts medicine at the top is beginning to crumble, helped by those on the inside as well as the outside.

The medical model of anxiety

The medical model of emotional distress divides disorders into anxiety (which might include insomnia), depression and psychotic illness. Doctors vary widely in the degree to which they use a medical model to understand distress or look at the problem from a psychological perspective. However the fact that a client is taking psychotropic drugs indicates some acceptance of a medical model by both client and doctor.

A consensus statement of the medical profession (Lader et al., 1992) sets out within the format of diagnosis, treatment and prognosis, to identify and describe anxiety, and defines it as: 'apprehensive expectation about two or more life circumstances' (1992: 560) with the symptoms described as 'worry plus somatic, affective, cognitive and behavioural symptoms which vary'. The borderline between normal and pathological anxiety is defined as when people seek advice and the warning is given that anxiety cannot be eliminated entirely. The 'life circumstances' are not referred to again and treatment focuses on symptom management not cure.

Although it is recognized that medication on its own may discourage people in their efforts to cope with anxiety in other ways, it is assumed that pharmacological and psychological therapies may be used alone or in combination. The assumption that the two are better than one on its own contributes to the medical view that drugs have a useful part to play in the treatment of anxiety, and that prescribing is not incompatible with counselling. Anti-anxiety drugs are treated as a single category with no differences identified in their psychological effects which might affect psychological therapies. Lader et al. (1992) do not have high expectations of psychological therapies since they regard some patients as not suitable, clinical psychologists and nurses as being in short supply and private sector counselling as being of uncertain quality. Therapies are seen as 'techniques' of a cognitive or behavioural nature and are mostly prescriptive rather than exploratory.

The consensus statement lists categories of drugs and when they should be used: for example, when depression is present or in order to remove symptoms which obstruct other treatment. If anxiety is severe, then drugs are seen as essential. Long-term treatment with drugs is not ruled out and there is acceptance that for people already dependent on benzodiazepines there is little else to do but continue to prescribe.

Four management stages are outlined according to the complexity of treatment and cover the initial intervention by the general practitioner; psychological management by general practitioner, nurse, clinical psychologist or psychiatrist who might provide one of the prescriptive therapies; the use of medication; and fourthly, specialist care which implies hospital admission. The management of anxiety remains firmly within a medical perspective and although their cooperation is sought and self-help books are advocated, patients have little role to play in diagnosis.

The medical view of depression

A consensus statement on the recognition and management of depression (Paykel and Priest, 1992: 1198) shows the way in which the group recognizes the internal experience, symptoms and mood which are classified as 'depression'. There is a brief acknowledgement that 'depressive disorders have a range of causes' but that 'what matters is presence of the syndrome'.

Treatment again focuses on managing symptoms and includes the role of antidepressants, psychosocial management, psychological treatments and psychiatric referral. There is an acceptance here that treating the marital difficulty, postnatal depression or social isolation as the underlying cause, with brief counselling or cognitive therapy is appropriate and effective. However there is some discrepancy in the two statements that 'Psychosocial and medication approaches combine well and should often be used together, and to some extent their targets are different' (1992: 1201).

Prescribing antidepressants is advised for major depressive episodes (they are less effective in mild depression) and 'should not be withheld because the depression seems understandable' (1992: 1200). So they are to be used 'irrespective of cause' although not in isolation in treatment. Drug therapy is advocated for four to six months after the initial stage to prevent relapse and advice is given on how to encourage the patient to comply.

Part of that advice is that antidepressants are not addictive or habit-forming. While this may be strictly true, since like other psychotropic drugs there is no evidence of the drugs being taken in ever-increasing doses or of craving, it omits to mention the evidence that patients may become dependent on antidepressants both physically and psychologically (*International Drug Therapy News*, 1984; Dilsaver 1989). The fact that they are taken in a lower dose at first to allow tolerance to the side-effects suggests the possibility of a withdrawal syndrome on abstinence.

Objective reality versus subjective experience

Medicine is assumed to be more concerned with 'objective reality' than 'subjective reality' and so focuses on the symptoms and mood changes that accompany psychological problems. The evidence for these is of course fairly subjective in itself and relies on accurate observation and reporting by the patient. In a book which argues against the medical model in psychiatry, Johnstone (1989: 241) points out that it 'operates on the assumption that there is a physical basis for mental illness although none has ever been found.

Johnstone makes the further point that 'its treatments lack a rationale for their effects and probably cause as much disability as they cure'. However there is a well-established approach in medicine that if the symptoms of disease are effectively removed then it can be assumed that the disease itself is probably being treated. Of course this is not universally applied, but it may influence the doctor towards treating symptoms which seem more tangible than the client's inner experience.

Emotional distress leads to biochemical changes in the brain since all thinking, feeling and behaviour is biochemically mediated. However the medical model assumes that it is the other way round and that the biochemical changes are causing the changes in thinking, feeling and behaviour and therefore that pharmacological treatments will lead to relief of distress. This bilateral relationship between distress and chemistry assumes that external factors of life experience, relationships and events will themselves be mitigated by the person's changed psychological state.

For example a person who is anxious will have a range of symptoms and will feel fear at the anticipation of some future experience and may take steps to avoid it. Drugs change the chemistry of the brain, decrease symptoms, reduce the anxious mood and therefore affect the person's thinking, feeling and behaviour. It is assumed that the person can therefore tackle his problem more effectively once the anxious mood is removed. The underlying assumption is not that anxiety is an inappropriate or undesirable state, but that it has no deeper meaning.

Social pressures

Social pressures determine what emotion it is appropriate for an individual to express and here *context* has a major influence. Women may be more likely to express sadness or fear while anger may be seen as more appropriate for men. The circumstances of a disaster or death make certain feelings noble and deserving of sympathy. Avoidant behaviour, addictions or breaking down in public are perceived as weak, evidence of poor coping and may be viewed as undeserving. Failure to live up to group norms may leave the individual ashamed and reluctant to disclose to others what is a perfectly normal reaction.

There is less shame in illness and a consultation with a doctor is a private affair when distress can be acknowledged more openly. Physical symptoms can seem more real and evidence that the origin of the problem is on the outside, just as infection is seen as invading the body. It may be more comfortable to think that the body or psyche is malfunctioning and needs to be put right, than to acknowledge that a person is responsible for himself and that the origin of the problem is on the inside.

People have been encouraged to believe that an emotionally pain-free existence is not only possible but what most other people are achieving. Life-style changes, digging up the past and coming to terms with who we really are take a great deal of time and effort with little guarantee of ultimate success. Handing over the problem to an expert carer, doing it quickly and effortlessly by taking drugs seems worth at least a try.

Doctors faced with a succession of patients who are unhappy, are exposed to a high level of emotional distress for which their training does not prepare them and from which their style of working does not protect them. A psychological assessment made in a few minutes as any other diagnosis, is still a hypothesis which can only be confirmed by effective treatment. Society's expectations that given sufficient training, research, resources and technology, doctors should be able to cure all illnesses conspire to discourage the doctor from admitting his or her ignorance or inability to cure. Given the doctor's commitment to do no harm, offering any help possible to relieve distress with drugs is seen as part of the treatment. Of course there are circumstances when prescribing may be the best available treatment, as in the control of psychotic illnesses such as schizophrenia, enabling the individual to lead a more normal life. Sometimes prescribing may relieve distress without complicating psychological functioning, as in the use of beta-blockers to control the physical symptoms of performance anxiety.

Unrealistic expectations

Expectations of what drugs can do have modified and more doctors are themselves using counselling approaches to good effect and widening the range of services available within the surgery. In the same way people are becoming more willing to seek counselling for themselves but are not always sure when drugs are necessary or helpful. However there will probably always be patients who are unwilling to use counselling and doctors who are not interested in counselling themselves who will feel they must do what they can to help. Ultimately decisions require the use of fine judgement on the part of patient and doctor and neither can be expected to be right all the time.

Several other treatments can be combined with drugs or used as alternatives. Within the health and social services these are usually behavioural therapies such as anxiety and stress management, or cognitive therapy particularly for depression. Counselling of a more exploratory kind is increasingly available either in surgeries or mental health resource centres or in other community settings. Understandably these therapies are usually brief and long-term or deeper approaches are more readily found in the private sector. All these approaches aim to go beyond the symptoms to identify and treat the cause.

Myths that some patients are not suitable for psychotherapy abound and have more to do with the suitability of the therapeutic approach or the therapist's flexibility than the patient. Of course a counsellor specializing in a single approach is unlikely to be able to help everybody, but that does not mean the patient cannot be helped. Some doctors are only aware of dynamic psychotherapy offered through psychiatry or privately and the kinds of therapies more widely available in the health service which are seen as lower-level 'techniques'.

Psychotropic drugs

Antipsychotics

Short-term use For severely disturbed patients in hospital and for severe anxiety.

Long-term use In low doses for anxiety, for schizophrenia and other psychoses. They should be withdrawn gradually.

Unwanted effects Sedation, dry mouth, blurred vision, constipation, sexual dysfunction, menstrual disturbances, dizziness, tremor, slowness, apathy, emotional withdrawal, agitation, restlessness, depression, palpitations, rashes.

Effectiveness Where patients have a schizophrenic illness antipsychotic drugs can be very effective in stabilizing emotions, thoughts and behaviour sufficiently to enable the person to live outside hospital. Once the optimum dose level has been found it is probably important from the medical point of view that the patient continues to take the drugs regularly since, although there may be periods when the condition seems well under control, there may be other periods when the patient experiences a worsening of all the symptoms and may need psychiatric admission again.

Psychiatric opinion seems to be fairly committed to the view that psychotic illness has a large genetic component which is exacerbated by social and environmental factors in early life. Since there is no psychiatric cure as yet for this organic deficit, the best that medicine can offer is to control the condition as far as possible with the minimum interference with the patient's life. The early stages of treatment are taken up with finding the optimum dose of psychotropic drugs which will be used to maintain the patient in the long term. In addition, patients are offered a range of social support and training in skills for living by social workers and may spend time in residential or day care centres which give continued support.

Limitations It is widely recognized that the blocking effects of the drugs make people cut off and unable to express feelings, affect thought processes and problem-solving, and make people passive. It is a major drawback of antipsychotic drugs that they may make the underlying condition almost inaccessible. This is the price which is paid for controlling the illness sufficiently to enable the individual to live in the community.

Antipsychotic drugs used in low doses for anxiety are not appropriate in the long term because the disadvantages of their side-effects far outweigh any advantage. Other treatments are available for anxiety and if there is no evidence of psychosis then their use is inadvisable. They have been used to 'aid' withdrawal from benzodiazepines when no psychological treatment was used to deal with the original problem, and some people may have continued with them for that reason.

Lithium

Use   For the treatment and prevention of mania, manic-depressive illness.
Blood levels require monitoring.

Unwanted effects   Nausea, drowsiness, tremor, muscle weakness.

Effectiveness   Long-term use of lithium is effective in damping down the manic phase of manic-depressive illness. If untreated in this way, people may have periods when their behaviour may seem bizarre to others and they may have unrealistic ideas and expectations. Regular use of lithium and careful monitoring are important since reducing or stopping the drug can precipitate another manic phase.

Limitations   The drugs do not discriminate between feelings and so all feelings are damped down, making people's emotional response seem inappropriate sometimes. The mania which is just held in check may seem to be trying to break through and there is an element of unpredictability about both response and behaviour which may destabilize relationships if the drug's effects are not understood. If the diagnosis was incorrect, then the disadvantages outweigh the advantages of using it, and patients can be withdrawn.

Antidepressants *(also known as tranquillisers / to anx)*

Use   For moderate to severe depression, anxiety and phobias, obsessional disorders, insomnia associated with depression, eating disorders. The dose is gradually increased over two to four weeks until the desired effect is achieved and to allow tolerance to the side-effects to develop. They are taken for three months to a year or more.
They should be withdrawn gradually.

Unwanted effects Sedation, dry mouth, blurred vision, constipation, sexual dysfunction, dizziness, nausea, palpitations, sweating, tremor, loss of or increase in appetite and weight gain, worsening depression, rashes, confusion, dependence.

Effectiveness People who are given antidepressants may be expected to take them for at least three months and possibly for a year. The drugs are used to control the symptoms until the depression remits with time. This long-term use is also seen as a measure to prevent the depression resurfacing. It is expected that people may have other periods in their lives when the depression comes back and the drugs can be reintroduced for another long course. Clearly if the underlying cause is not being treated then the depression can re-occur.

When people are severely depressed and dysfunctional, that is doing very little, staying in bed, barely eating or engaging with others, then antidepressants have an important function in lifting the depressed feelings enough for people to start functioning again. When depression is this severe other therapies cannot be effective and may be unable to hold the client sufficiently to prevent suicidal attempts or a psychotic-like state. Very severe depression makes people inaccessible to therapy or counselling.

Limitations For mild to moderate depression antidepressants may have little beneficial effect and may make the depression much worse. This may be because the depression is in some way helping to protect the person from much worse feelings which are exposed when the depression lifts a little. The removal of this protective effect may worsen the depression leading to suicidal thoughts or attempts. Antidepressants are themselves toxic in overdose or may be used in conjunction with alcohol in suicide attempts.

Antidepressants have a sedative effect which is useful when insomnia is associated with depression, and may play a part in their use for anxiety, phobias and obsessional states. It is important to see that a symptom is being treated and not to think that these conditions are in any way being appropriately treated. It is much more obvious in the case of their use for eating disorders when depression may be part of the overall psychological picture but is not the focus of treatment.

Psychological therapies can be started while people are still taking the drugs and in the case of very severe depression the drugs may make counselling possible. People can begin to explore the underlying meaning of their depression but are likely, while on the drugs, to benefit first from approaches targeted at cognitive and behavioural functioning. As drugs are being reduced, or if the depression is not severe, counselling can proceed but will not be complete until all the suppressed issues have surfaced after drugs are stopped.

Benzodiazepines

Uses Anxiety: 'for the short-term relief (two to four weeks only) of anxiety that is severe, disabling or subjecting the individual to unacceptable distress' (*British National Formulary*, s. 4.1); panic attacks, muscle relaxation, stress.

Insomnia: for 'insomnia only when it is severe, disabling or subjecting the individual to extreme distress' (*British National Formulary*, s. 4.1).

They can be used on a daily basis or intermittently and should always be withdrawn gradually.

Unwanted effects Nausea, constipation, headache, tinnitus, dizziness, sexual dysfunction, tiredness, drowsiness, lethargy, poor concentration, impaired memory, anxiety, depression, agoraphobia, panic attacks, aggressive outbursts, dependence.

Effectiveness As both anxiolytics and hypnotics, benzodiazepines are very effective in sedating, relaxing muscles, blocking emotions, preventing memory processing and recall, and reducing activity of all kinds. They are non-selective in that most effects are likely, not just desired ones. They have a quick effect, producing sedation after 30 minutes and their effects last from between two hours to seven days.

Benzodiazepines are useful for their anticonvulsant properties either for epilepsy (clobazam) or to prevent fits during alcohol detoxification treatment (chlordiazepoxide for 14 days). They are sometimes continued for longer to prevent people restarting drinking since they can be controlled by the prescriber whereas alcohol is 'self-prescribed'. This harm-reduction use is not to be preferred to treating the underlying reason for excessive alcohol use.

The amnesic effects are useful in both surgery and dentistry where single doses may be used to sedate. Within a hospital setting they have other uses which would not apply outside, but the undesirable side of not being able to recall events and experiences might still cause people problems later. Some of the amnesic effects are removed once the drugs are stopped.

Limitations Tolerance to the drugs can occur quite quickly, especially if they are used on a regular basis or for periods outside the guidelines. It is their use and effectiveness for emotional problems which make them difficult to stop after short courses. They appear to be a solution and if dependence is acceptable or seen as more bearable than the distress, they may become a drug of long-term use since they discourage real and often more painful solutions.

Since tolerance does occur, the drugs cease to have beneficial effect after four months' continual use (Committee on the Review of Medicines, 1980) and probably after a much shorter time for hypnotics. However people will also have become psychologically dependent and may have unrealistic beliefs about the drugs' continued effects.

Benzodiazepines have a complex withdrawal syndrome (Hammersley and Hamlin, 1990), which cannot be accurately predicted except by making a trial reduction to see if symptoms occur. Since the likelihood is that people will be dependent if they have been taking them for periods outside the guidelines, or even within them, the drugs should always be withdrawn very slowly. Long-term use and higher doses affect the severity of the withdrawal syndrome which has both physical and psychological symptoms easily mistaken for something else.

This group of drugs makes people therapeutically inaccessible even on low doses, since the drugs interfere with thinking and concentration and make people emotionally withdrawn and passive. Sometimes they have a paradoxical effect of making people more excited and less inhibited, particularly when used with alcohol. The drugs can sometimes make people difficult to engage, especially if drugs have been taken over a long period of time.

Beta-blockers

Use Short-term for performance-related anxiety, stress or as an alternative to benzodiazepines. Also for angina, high blood pressure, irregular heart rhythms.

Unwanted effects Dizziness, cold hands and feet, fatigue, sleep disturbance, nightmares, asthma.
They do not have to be withdrawn gradually.

Effectiveness All beta-blockers slow the heart and therefore are effective to treat some of the symptoms of anxiety such as palpitations and tremor as well as having a medical use for hypertension.

They are also used for the prevention of migraine which might be considered a psychological symptom.

Limitations   They have no effect on anxiety itself, although their effectiveness in masking symptoms might lead people to believe they have. There is an important psychological message in their prescribing. They do not directly interfere with counselling.

Other sedatives – buspirone

Use   For anxiety, as an alternative to benzodiazepines (same guidelines). It takes two weeks to become effective.

Unwanted effects   Nausea, dizziness, headache, nervousness, light-headedness, excitement, slow heart rate, palpitations, chest pain, drowsiness, confusion, dry mouth, fatigue, sweating.

Other sedatives – zopiclone

Use   For insomnia, as an alternative to benzodiazepines (same guidelines).

Unwanted effects   Mild bitter metallic after-taste, nausea, irritability, confusion, depression, drowsiness, rashes, dizziness, light-headedness, impaired judgement and coordination.
They should both be withdrawn gradually.

Dependence
A client taking prescribed psychotropic drugs who comes for counselling may be dependent on them physically and/or psychologically. Counsellors and prescribers should take this into consideration along with the client's wishes, when giving advice or offering other services. Drugs whether wanted or not, may be the best available treatment for some psychotic conditions or for epilepsy, so 'need' may override preference. Here long-term dependence may be acceptable.

However when prescribed drugs are one of the options in treatment and alternatives are available and acceptable, no sudden change in treatment is safe until dependence issues have been considered. It is important to recognize that prescribing for dependence is necessary for drugs which need gradual withdrawal, such as benzodiazepines and antidepressants. Although the drugs may no longer be having a beneficial effect they are still having an effect in preventing withdrawal symptoms and that is a crucially important use.

Dependence may be given as a reason for not offering other treatments which might be used with drugs or as an alternative. Dealing with the dependence may require expert help but the alternatives can be sought from a wide variety of sources professional and voluntary, statutory and private. The consensus statements appear to suggest that the medical profession has very little knowledge of psychological therapies and counselling (in spite of being advised by clinical psychologists) and little faith in practitioners other than statutory ones. Fortunately this is not always the case.

There are legal implications for the prescriber in both continuing to prescribe or withdraw drugs. It may come as a surprise to some counsellors to discover that prescribing outside the guidelines (*British National Formulary*), and the drug's licence, will not leave the prescriber open to legal sanction. Failure to prescribe for dependence, abrupt withdrawal or re-prescribing after the person has withdrawn following a previous period of dependence, might be seen as negligence. However a failure to monitor drug use or to give appropriate warnings or advice is less easy to prove, and the patient also has some responsibility in this.

Just as drugs are seen to have benefits in terms of being a low-cost, quick and easily administered form of treatment, when dependence occurs these same reasons can be used to justify doing nothing. Withdrawal of drugs or alternatives such as counselling are thought to be expensive, take a long time to obtain and take effect, and not to be suitable for some people. The option of doing nothing which was discounted when the drugs were first prescribed may be seen as the best treatment when people are dependent. Sociological factors can be seen to influence these decisions.

The psychological message of prescribing

Prescribing antipsychotics gives the patient the message that he has a serious mental illness which is genetic in origin, exacerbated by factors in early life and for which there is no known cure. The emphasis of treatment is on 'management'; that is controlling the symptoms so that the patient can live as normal a life as possible in the community, with time in hospital if he is at risk of harming himself or other people.

It is assumed that there may be no improvement in the illness but that the patient can benefit from support and social or life-skills training and education. When these drugs are prescribed for anxiety in low dose it is often because the prescriber thinks the anxiety is so severe that 'we must hit it hard on the head' and a more serious drug will guarantee success; failure of the treatment implies that the anxiety has 'got out of control'.

Prescribing lithium for extreme mood swings from severe depression to mania suggests that the moods are out of control and that modifying them will help the patient to fit in socially without displaying extremes of behaviour. Bi-polar depression is seen as more severe and recurrent and therefore treatment with lithium will always be needed to control it. Again the patient receives a message that he is ill and that no other treatment is available.

Although aetiological distinctions between reactive and endo-genous depression are no longer thought to be important it is still the message of prescribing antidepressants that drugs are the first choice treatment for an illness. Sometimes people are told that it is caused by biochemical changes in the brain or is a personality defect, often not in so many words. 'Some people are just more vulnerable to depression, particularly if it is already in the family.' This is a large hint that there is a genetic link although it could equally be due to learned responses and family dynamics.

A less pejorative message is that 'anybody can get it – sometimes it just comes out of the blue for no good reason'. In this case the prescribing gives the message that ill fortune is to blame and antidepressants are just like antibiotics, deservedly given to relieve suffering. A strong suggestion here is that suffering is unnecessary and undesirable and serves no useful purpose.

Exhibiting feelings, especially crying, is frequently seen as 'not coping' and benzodiazepines have often been the preferred treat-ment for this and confirm the diagnosis. Another message is that it is not good for an individual to be 'upset' or angry and therefore he needs help. The person may in fact have been encouraged to seek help from the prescriber because someone else thinks he needs help or does not want to be exposed to his feelings. There is also the message that people do not need to have bad feelings since these can be suppressed by drugs.

Prescribing may be a way of discouraging people from trying psychological therapies:

'It is unwise to dig too deeply into yourself/your psyche/your unconscious.'
'You may not like what you find.'
'You may not be able to cope with what you discover.'
'That sort of treatment can make you worse.'
'It is a waste of time exploring yourself, here is a quick cure.'

'That sort of thing is alright for some people' (i.e. not you).
'Your symptoms are what trouble you.'
'Symptoms can be harmlessly removed.'
'If the symptoms are removed, then you will not worry about
them, and that will be an improvement or at least stop you
getting worse.'

Something is better than nothing
A consultation is more readily seen as unsatisfactory by both
doctor and patient, if there is no tangible outcome. Doctors are
accustomed to giving reassurance and allaying fears, prescribing a
treatment or making a referral at the end of every consultation and
this conforms to the patient's expectations too. Prescribing is part
of this important ritual and fits with the belief that the doctor's job
is to *do* something.

PSYCHOLOGICAL MESSAGES
Some of the messages which are conveyed by this ritual are
sometimes or partly true and sometimes not. They include:

'Doing nothing may make things worse.'
'This will help/make some improvement.'
'It can do no harm and may do some good.'
'We shall have to try it and see.'
'You should let an expert tell you what is wrong and make you
better.'
'Allow the doctor to do his/her job.'
'Prescribing is a scientific treatment which is therefore reliable.'
'Drugs are highly researched and getting better all the time.'
'Technological advances in medicine mean that drugs are more
specific and more problem-free.'
'Your doctor knows best.'
'Doctors are educated and trained to a higher standard than
anyone else.'

The patient's part in the consultation
People consulting doctors whether in general practice or in hospital,
start from a position of wanting help with a problem or symptoms.
They are consulting an expert who may have knowledge or skill
which can help them find some relief and that is what many people
are seeking. Prescribing is a perfectly proper part of the help which
is offered but the line which divides help from 'Rescuing' is a very
fine – or perhaps a very blurred – one. On the wrong side of that
line is the situation where the patient is implicitly handing over

responsibility for himself to someone else to take care of. In illness that may be appropriate, but when problems have a psychological basis rather than a physical one, it is dangerous. The shift in power and responsibility implies:

'It's nothing to do with me.'
'Other people understand me better than I do.'
'It is up to you to change how I feel or make me better.'
'I'm ill.'
'I need something outside myself (medicine) to make me feel better again.'
'You take over.'

There are some situations or problems which are primarily of psychological origin which do require the doctor to take over care, prescribe or admit to hospital, and that blurs the boundaries even further. For example people in psychotic episodes, under the influence of alcohol or drugs, in severe depression or with suicidal feelings, may need that kind of immediate medical help.

The opposite difficulty can arise when a person who recognizes that he has a psychological problem is reluctant or unwilling to take drugs or accept psychiatric help at all. Perhaps, in order to maintain control, the person sees it as vital that he only uses drugs as a last resort even at the risk of psychotic relapses. This may involve the doctor in 'persuading' the patient to comply with what is being recommended for his care.

The patient's beliefs about drugs
Over-optimism about how useful drugs are in psychological treatments can make people very reluctant to look for or accept an alternative view. Examples of these beliefs are:

'Drugs are a cure for my illness.'
'My illness is so severe that I need drugs.'
'I could not manage without drugs.'
'If my doctor has prescribed them they must be what I need.'
'I'm sure they are (still) doing me some good.'
'I'm not crazy, I'm sick.'
'When I'm better, I'll be able to stop taking the drugs.'
'I know they are not a cure but they really help me cope.'
'I'd go crazy without drugs.'
'They are much more effective than just talking about things.'
'They replace a chemical that my brain hasn't got enough of.'

Underestimating the usefulness of drugs occurs when people could get some benefit or actually really need them; for instance, when they are dependent on them. Examples of these beliefs are:

'Drugs mess you up.'
'All I get is a prescription – nobody will listen to me.'
'I expected the doctor to tell me what to do not give me a prescription.'
'I know I've got a real illness but they don't believe me.'
'I can stop taking these drugs any time I like.'
'I only took them because the doctor wanted me to.'
'Only weak people take drugs.'
'If I could get off these drugs, all my problems would be solved.'

Pharmacological solutions

Once a pharmacological solution has been selected even for a trial period, it is more difficult for the prescriber to stop. For example if a drug is being used for a trial, when does the trial stop, and what happens if the patient does not want to stop? How is effectiveness to be measured, and by whom? All drugs have unwanted effects, but who decides whether these are acceptable or not? Will the doctor attempt to remove the side-effects by further prescribing? Do the psychological side-effects then become part of the diagnosis?

Confusing this issue is the 'placebo effect' by which the benefit is actually due to the doctor's and patient's expectations and the care and attention which accompany the prescribing. It is possible to demonstrate this effect in an experiment but not to measure it in real-life situations. Of course the effectiveness of a placebo has real benefits for the patient which should not be discounted. The benefits to the patient may be ascribed to the pharmacological effect rather than the placebo and this encourages further prescribing.

This is part of the reason why drugs are prescribed outside the guidelines; for example when benzodiazepines are prescribed routinely or beyond four weeks. It is the fact that the patient experiences a benefit even if only short-term relief of symptoms, that encourages the doctor to continue prescribing. It would be very strange to hear a doctor say 'I am so pleased you found the drugs helped, but I am not going to prescribe any more because they are not *really* helping you.' How would the doctor justify the first prescription then?

A second reason why drugs are continued is that prescribing one drug encourages reliance on others. For example if antipsychotic drugs are used to control hallucinations, it is appropriate to prescribe an anti-Parkinsonism drug for the shakiness which is a side-effect. In the same way, benzodiazepines cause depression which can then be treated with antidepressants and so on. This approach can lead to multiple prescribing or 'polypharmacy' where each drug is added to remove the effects of the previous one. Rarely are drugs subtracted; they are usually added. Nor do diagnostic hypotheses get rejected; more often they become part of a life-long drug trial.

Psychological side-effects of drugs such as depression, phobias, obsessions, increased anxiety, disinhibition and others are often not ascribed to the drugs effects but are seen as part of the underlying illness. This is well recognized in some cases. For example when patients complained of increased anxiety on abruptly stopping benzodiazepines, the anxiety was thought to be due not to a withdrawal effect but to a resurfacing or exacerbation of the original anxiety.

Once the doctor has prescribed, if the patient then seems to get worse, not only may new drugs be added but the choice of drug may well be influenced: 'If anxiety increases, then raise the dose until you have the condition under control.' Many psychotropic drugs actually do make the condition worse and so levels of drug use go up and doctors may be more emphatic about the necessity of taking drugs. Antipsychotic drugs used inappropriately are examples of this.

The doctor as counsellor

Just as some counsellors can be rigidly opposed to prescribing, so some doctors can be rigidly opposed to counselling. However few people in either profession take such an extreme view and there is a growing movement within medicine advocating counselling within the practice and by the doctor as well as by others. Through study and experience, many doctors have picked up a good understanding of psychological issues and practice, and some have gone on to train in counselling skills.

Whether they offer counselling themselves or refer to others, doctors are the key people in managing a shift from prescribing to counselling. They hold the power to prescribe or not, and having demonstrated concern and care for the patient they can suggest the move towards seeking counselling. Regular consultations offer the doctor repeated opportunities to increase the patient's motivation to use counselling either with drugs or as an alternative. It is the doctor who can encourage the hope of dealing with the underlying issue rather than managing the symptoms.

Counselling by doctors is not free from problems and difficulties. Apart from the conflict between the two roles, insufficient training and lack of supervision, doctors finding themselves stretched beyond their competence may resort to prescribing again. This may give the patient a message that he is very difficult to treat, that he has not lived up to the doctor's expectations and that counselling has failed.

Conclusion

While a medical model does acknowledge that past experience and current events play a part in the aetiology of psychological distress, its focus is primarily on management rather than cure. The purpose of prescribing is therefore the reduction of symptoms, the suppression of feelings, the control of thinking and the management of behaviour. It is relatively successful at achieving these objectives in the short term with a ratio of benefit to cost which many find acceptable.

What prescribing does not and cannot do is deal with the underlying issue or cause. Although the past cannot be changed, the meaning that a person gives to his past can be modified through therapeutic methods such as counselling. Physical symptoms which are suppressed get stronger because their purpose is to indicate that something in the person's life needs attention. As drugs are used in the longer term the cost of taking drugs may outweigh the benefits which begin to show themselves to be mostly superficial. People need to be aware of this and the implications of accepting drugs as all or part of their treatment.

Counsellors who work with people taking drugs may assume that the drugs are part of the solution rather than part of the problem to be assessed. Being ignorant of drugs and unaware of the implications of drug use, counsellors may not allow for it in the assessment of the client, the problem and the objectives of counselling. Counsellors may be tempted to overestimate how much doctors understand drugs and their skill in diagnosis and assume that there is nothing to be challenged. The medical model is not the only way that people and their emotional distress can be viewed and the next chapter looks at a different standpoint.

2
The Counselling Perspective

A psychological model

The British Association for Counselling (1989) describes counselling as:

> the skilled and principled use of relationship to facilitate self-knowledge, emotional acceptance and growth, and the optimal development of personal resources. The overall aim is to provide an opportunity to work towards living more satisfyingly and resourcefully. Counselling . . . may be concerned with developmental issues, addressing and resolving specific problems, making decisions, coping with crisis, developing personal insights and knowledge, working through feelings of inner conflict or improving relationships with others.

There is nothing here about symptoms because a psychological model of emotional distress assumes that anxiety and depression are about something in the person's life. Furthermore from this perspective the disorder itself is therapeutic, since by putting out distress signals, such as symptoms and changes in mood and behaviour, the disorder provokes the individual to make adjustments in his understanding of self, relationships or life. It is by investigating these manifestations of distress that the person and the counsellor seek to make sense of the inner world of experience rather than regarding the person as ill or malfunctioning.

There is a difference between this model and the medical model (see Chapter 1) in terms of the direction of causality (Figure 2.1). A psychological model assumes that the interaction between past experience, relationships and current events and the client's thinking, feeling and behaviour leads to the outcome of mood change and symptoms. It recognizes that illness or drugs may be alternative explanations but if these can be excluded, it sees the client's internal reality as the cause of the symptoms. The medical model sees illness as the primary cause of symptoms leading to changes in behaviour thinking and feelings, which interact with the person's relationships, current events and past experience.

This leads to different conclusions about what the options are.

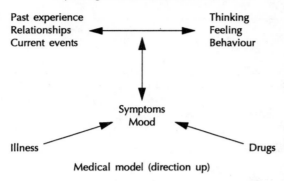

Figure 2.1 *Difference between the psychological and medical models*

Instead of seeing treatment objectives as being about the removal of distress, counsellors recognize that feelings of distress may be appropriate, unavoidable or even acceptable especially if time-limited. Keeping the symptoms and distress enables people in counselling to confront the underlying issues, work through them while processing them emotionally and find resolution and acceptance. This approach accepts that life will continue to include painful experiences as well as joyful ones but that showing the pain is evidence of coping rather than a failure to cope.

This difference of approach (see Table 2.1) shows why counselling and drug treatments are sometimes incompatible. A medical model of causality approaches the individual in physical terms focusing on the biochemical mechanisms by which all psychological processes are mediated. The illness can be viewed as a disequilibrium which can be restored by drugs and leads to the view that some people may need to take drugs for the rest of their lives in order to maintain this. It removes the need to confront the inner psychological reality which may prove a more painful and difficult process even if it leads to a more fundamental and long-term solution.

Once the cause of the symptoms has been identified as primarily of psychological origin rather than due to organic illness, then the counselling perspective defines the treatment model. Johnstone (1989: 288), in her critique of psychiatry, states as her conclusion that 'ultimately we need to move away from, and eventually abandon the whole medical model approach which . . . underlies all the other flaws in psychiatry'.

Table 2.1 *Differences in treatment and outcome of medical and counselling models*

	Symptoms	
	↙ Medical model	↘ Counselling model
First consultation	Illness diagnosed	Underlying issue identified
Treatment	Drugs prescribed	Exploration of inner reality
Short-term outcome	Symptoms relieved Emotions suppressed	Increased distress Decline in symptoms
Long-term outcome	Underlying problem unchanged Increased symptoms	Underlying problem resolved Symptom relief

Psychosocial problems once identified, require the doctor to switch from using the medical model towards using a counselling model because treating symptoms may lead to their removal in the short term but to their increase in the long term. As the symptoms are suppressed they may get worse, more numerous or surface in some other form. If the doctor is still following the medical model it will be easy to believe that there is a secondary condition or that the illness is getting worse requiring further drug treatment.

One factor which makes identifying the origin of the symptoms difficult is that psychosocial problems may take about two years before they produce sufficiently troublesome symptoms to lead a person to seek a consultation with a doctor. Both may discount or never consider that life events so far in the past are the cause of the symptoms. Where psychosocial factors relating to the person's early experiences or long-term relationships are producing the symptoms, they may never consider this because they are looking for something the doctor can treat.

Combining the medical and counselling models

The effect on the client

Whatever the counsellor's background and approach, the fact that the client is taking prescribed drugs is a significant factor in the whole process. There is a third party who has already made an intervention by prescribing even if its relevance is not seen by the client who is coming for counselling. The third party is not fully present or acknowledged in the relationship although he or she is affecting it. This may be true even if drugs have been prescribed for some other reason than the one currently being dealt with in counselling.

A client who is coming for counselling who has already been prescribed drugs by his general practitioner, may think it so commonplace as not to be remarkable or worth telling the counsellor. Either the client thinks the drugs were necessary for some totally separate condition which is none of the counsellor's business, or they were prescribed to help the problem being brought to the counsellor. In either case they can safely be ignored since they would not have been prescribed other than appropriately. Here the counsellor is at best the second person from whom help is being sought and the client has already accepted the first person's help or solution.

The client has already been helped by having symptoms reduced so to some extent may be less motivated to search for real and possibly more painful solutions. The prescribing which precedes or accompanies the counselling will undermine it unless the reason for it is made very clear and the limits of pharmacological interventions are acknowledged. This may be the case when antipsychotic drugs are given to control severe psychosis, or when antidepressants are given to alleviate severe depression in order for counselling to be possible. However the giving of benzodiazepine hypnotics for insomnia will make the search for the cause of the insomnia more difficult and the client less able to tell when the cause has been identified.

Not every client who comes for counselling is coming entirely for himself. He may have been referred by his general practitioner or consultant, teacher or tutor, supervisor or manager, relative or friend because that person believes that counselling may be appropriate. He may have been sent, or required to seek therapeutic help because an institution or organization makes it a condition of continued employment or training, as part of a sentence or disciplinary decision. Some people may seek counselling in order to keep things as they are, not to make fundamental changes.

Many people are motivated to seek counselling as part of their search for the relief of symptoms both physical and emotional; that is in order to get better. They may really see their problem as a medical one even if they have some inkling that psychological factors underpin it. Drugs are often a very effective 'quick fix' and if a medical opinion has been sought first, prescribing may have occurred. Some problems of this kind have often been successfully 'managed' for many years before they have become severe enough for another approach to be considered. Anxiety, insomnia, depression, phobias and obsessions all come into this category.

Clients may come to counselling because they have a particular problem or are in a crisis or are dealing with life transitions. Here they are likely to be looking for expert advice and guidance or somebody who understands things better or knows how they ought to be. People who have experienced a bereavement, particularly a traumatic one, or a crisis where the cause is easily identified and where an instant response seems to be called for, are likely to have been offered 'something to tide you over' for immediate relief of distress. It is very tempting for prescribers to 'give something to guarantee a good night's sleep'. Such explanations can sound plausible.

Counselling which has a strong educational component when social or communication skills are being taught or where the client recognizes that he needs to learn some assertiveness skills or techniques, shares the same prescriptive approach. Cognitive and behavioural therapies and many short-term therapies are mainly prescriptive rather than exploratory, and are often combined with prescribing since the client is expecting the counsellor to 'do something with or to me'. Here the client wants the counsellor to help him change his thinking, feelings and behaviour.

Counselling which seeks to listen to, understand and explore the client's view of his world, or where the client expresses what he is looking for in terms of working at depth, personal development or growth is seen as more long term. Because it may take a long time it is tempting for the prescriber to offer a short-term solution in the form of drugs to accompany the counselling in the belief that when the problem is resolved the prescribing will no longer be needed. Since the prescribing can prevent the problem being resolved, it can lead to 'no-exit' therapy.

Sometimes the client is coming for counselling because he is demonstrating to some other person that he is 'trying', and of course going to fail. This may occur when the client is the designated 'sick one' or family scapegoat and long-term prescribing may have confirmed this. At some level the client realizes that to really engage with the counselling process may be too disturbing of the family dynamics, and the prescribing is a way to sabotage it. Outright refusal would seem ungrateful or uncooperative so the client agrees to 'try' with the expectation and hope of failure. This may be a way of expressing anger or punishing others.

Some clients are very sure, rightly or wrongly, about the kind of therapy that they are looking for, while others may be prepared to take anything on offer indiscriminately. An attitude of 'the more the merrier' encourages prescribers to give drugs a try to see if they work, and of course in one sense they usually do. In fact the client may be encouraged by a *laissez-faire* general practitioner to 'try them all and make up your own mind', or 'we'll hit it with everything to be on the safe side', by a cautious one.

So the client on prescribed drugs may be coming for a variety of reasons. Drugs may be necessary but the client may secretly be hoping that this is not so and clutching at straws, or willing to accept that view and be prepared to do what he can through counselling. He may have used drugs for a while, but now be looking for an alternative approach, wanting to reduce and come off the drugs if counselling can replace what the drugs were doing. Clients will vary and include those with a good knowledge and understanding of drug issues, along with those who are totally unaware that the drugs have any significance for their counselling.

The effect on the counsellor
The counsellor may be limited by the person or organization she works for in what she is allowed to do. There may be constraints of time and money, making short-term interventions all that is offered. The style of counselling may be limited to telephone work or in groups. The organization may have a policy which narrows the focus of counselling to work issues or the course being studied. Voluntary and charitable organizations may limit the scope of counselling to a single issue such as bereavement, or marriage or a disability.

Even with greater freedom, the counsellor will be limited by her level of competence, skills, knowledge and experience. Including drug issues in what is offered may compromise the counsellor in her employment when there is a conflict of roles. For example it may be difficult to offer counselling as a practice nurse or practice counsellor if the practice does not have an appropriate and consistent policy on prescribing psychotropic drugs or is not aware of the need for one. Counselling in a hospital setting may be restricted to not challenging the views of the medical consultant.

Counsellors in social work settings whether in residential, community centres or in the home, may have to accept the medical hierarchy even if they reject the medical model. Many of the clients being counselled in residential settings will also be attending outpatient clinics at the local hospital where they will be receiving drugs after little or no consultation with the counsellor. This is rarely a joint approach; the counsellor is expected to work alongside the prescribing. Much the same happens in day centres and with clients who are seen at home. The counselling is sub-ordinate to the prescribing.

When counselling takes place in the workplace perhaps by personnel or staff welfare workers, it may be assumed that any problem that has first been treated by a doctor is therefore a medical one. In the same way, counsellors in educational settings are so far removed from a medical setting that it might not occur to them that what they offer to the client may be limited by help elsewhere. Splitting the counselling and prescribing makes a clear distinction between what is a medical problem and what is a problem suitable for counselling even when no such distinction exists.

Drug agencies may be limited in what they offer to the client by their need to stay on good terms with doctors. They may require referral from a general practitioner or an assessment by a psychiatrist before accepting a client for counselling. The issue of drugs is then handed back to the doctor. Some agencies will offer counselling but are reluctant to go beyond their brief of offering 'support' during drug withdrawal for fear of getting it wrong.

The counsellor who also prescribes such as a psychiatrist, general practitioner or NHS psychotherapist, can find themselves in the worst of situations with the power to sabotage their own work! To which view of the problem do they subscribe? Either they trust their therapeutic skills and prescribe when necessary or as a last resort, or they try to separate their patients into different categories. Neither position is very easy and clients will be quick to pick up ambivalence, either being undermined by it or exploiting it.

The counsellor is not offering a solution in which the client plays no part. It is assumed that client and counsellor will work together but that the client will be doing most of the work. It is also assumed that at some level the client has the answer even if in his unconscious mind, through exploring the options or changing the client's thinking or behaviour. Above all the counsellor is offering the client the belief that the client makes sense: not that he has gone wrong.

The counselling view of emotional distress

As with a medical consultation, the client starts by defining what is wrong and may also start with a list of symptoms. However rather than a quick assessment and diagnosis (which is a working hypothesis) by the doctor, the client is encouraged to develop some working hypotheses. The counsellor offers to listen, to reflect back what is being said, to clarify, to summarize, to point out inconsistencies, to unearth beliefs, to point out unknown motives and consequences. All the client's behaviour, thinking and feelings both within and outside the consultation, are considered relevant.

One major purpose of counselling is to re-frame the medical diagnosis from a more psychological perspective. Anxiety is not seen as a set of symptoms but as a fearful response to something which has thoughts, feelings and behavioural components. It is assumed to be appropriate, to make sense, even if the circumstances which give rise to the anxiety are not in the present but in the client's past. Nor does it matter how other people would experience it; what matters is the client's subjective experience since he can work with nothing else.

Similarly depression is re-framed not as an illness or a bio-chemical imbalance, but as being 'about something'. All thinking, feeling, behaviour and mood changes come about as a result of biochemical changes, since humans are biochemical beings. Conversely all thinking, feeling, behaviour and mood changes affect the person's biochemical balance, and it is not possible to understand this complex process by determining which is the 'chicken' and which the 'egg'. In very general terms a pharmaceutical solution aims to change the biochemistry and symptoms and hence mood, whereas counselling works from the client's inner world to change mood and hence remove symptoms.

The counsellor offers the client the chance to explore his whole self and the part that events and relationships both past and present are still playing in his life in order to make sense of his depression, anxiety or insomnia. Since the client makes sense and emotional distress means something, it is not something to be eradicated. In other words emotional distress is much more than the symptoms of it. This approach assumes that what matters to start with is how the client perceives things, since his subjective reality is all there is for the client to work on. Objective reality may be sought later and this may or may not be achievable. Perhaps all he can hope for is a different subjective reality.

The meaning of symptoms

If people had no symptoms it would be difficult to know that something was wrong. They alert people to the fact that something in their bodies is wrong and the body that something in their lives is wrong. Quite often that message is well known but ignored and it is the increase in the number or severity of symptoms that ensures that attention is paid to them. The symptoms provide a focus of attention since they indicate some form of inner conflict or evidence of defence systems being activated. They signal the need to stop what is currently engaging the person's attention in order to redirect that attention to self-preservation.

Symptoms are also the means by which the client defines his problem; a way of making it accessible and available to someone else. He may start by describing physical symptoms instead of saying how he feels; he may say how he thinks he is functioning before he can say how he feels about it. Quite often the physical symptoms may express through metaphor what the client is not yet fully aware of. The symptoms help put the counsellor in touch with what is wrong and make contact with the problem from the client's perspective and experience.

Most people have a variety of symptoms either all the time or from time to time and pay little or no attention to them. Therefore the importance of the symptoms to the client is that he notices them. It may be because the usual pattern has changed and a symptom is there all the time instead of coming and going. The symptoms come in clusters which collectively have a special meaning. If the symptoms can be easily understood in terms of being causally related to some experience or event they may be tolerated even if quite severe.

Finding the meaning of symptoms provides the counsellor with the means of access to the problem that the client brings, whether it is what the client first thought it was or not. The meaning found may provoke both client and counsellor to see that the client's original understanding was in some sense inaccurate or not the whole picture. Symptoms may point out the significance of the wider context as they may be seen as a form of silent communication to others.

The history of the symptoms with their increases and decreases or temporary disappearance, provides a pattern of the progress of the problem as well as giving an indication of time-scale. Many clients have too short a time-scale expecting the origin of the problem to be found immediately before the onset of symptoms. Looking two or three years before the onset of symptoms may be more profitable as it allows for the time needed for the repressed feelings to work themselves out in physical form.

Counsellors attach other significance to symptoms by asking what the symptoms prevent or allow the client to do. In terms of prevention, the counsellor must ask herself and the client what the client is prevented from knowing, thinking, feeling or doing by the symptoms. The importance may be in what the client with symptoms is allowed which he might not be otherwise. This might include an opportunity to be listened to, get attention or recognition, express unmet needs, a way to ask for care or support or a way of expressing feelings unacceptable to others.

Sometimes the significance of the symptoms is revealed by asking what it might mean to the client to be rid of the symptoms, and that might mean further losses rather than a gain. It may be very important to the client to hold onto his symptoms as a means of defining himself, and until a greater sense of the self is established the symptoms may actually increase with every attempt to remove them. This is part of the reason why drugs which are for symptom removal often make 'the condition' appear worse.

The final purpose of the symptoms is that they act as a measure of progress in the treatment and in counselling. Whereas the client might expect an immediate change in the symptoms if drugs are being taken, changes of symptomatology may be more gradual and prolonged in counselling. This is because the symptoms are not usually being treated directly but abate because they no longer serve any useful purpose. They are an important indication of real progress and can be expected to stay away once the treatment is stopped, unlike symptoms which recur when drugs are stopped because the drugs were merely masking the problem.

Progress in counselling is often intermittent with periods of stuckness and getting blocked. Symptoms often indicate to clients that this is happening when they might not otherwise be aware that a re-think is needed. Some symptoms only occur when progress is being made. For example dreaming about a dead person following a bereavement may indicate that the mourning is progressing. Crying and expressing feelings can indicate progress, even if they were formerly defined as part of the problem itself.

The use of drugs

Beliefs about drugs
Doctors, counsellors and clients vary in their attitudes to drugs, some unrealistically believing that, even if drugs have some problems, research is working towards being able to provide a pill for every emotional problem. Some equally unrealistically, believe that drugs are always harmful and that everyone should have unlimited access to counselling whenever they need or want it. Finding a middle position is much harder without clear-cut rules and requires difficult judgements which are more easily identified when wrong.

Understanding the psychological effects of prescribing, taking or working with drugs is as important if not more important than knowing about the pharmacology. This is the area in which the doctor, client and counsellor are often united in their ignorance but unaware of it. It is easy to assume that doctors know more about drugs than when, how and what to prescribe. It is also easy to assume that drugs will do the client no psychological harm and may do some good. It is frequently assumed that drugs and counselling are just different approaches and are compatible. However, apart from the effects of the drugs themselves, the whole counselling approach is subtly undermined.

Drugs act on the symptoms and change how people think, feel and behave thereby affecting the counselling process. Drugs may also create dependence both physically and psychologically, because they may 'work too well', and may discourage the search for real solutions. Drugs can affect the counsellor's access to the client and the problem, keeping them 'just out of reach' so that the client seems poorly motivated or cut off and the problem vague or deeply buried.

Effects of psychotropic drugs

1 *On thinking*: loss of memories, poor recall of memory, poor concentration, confusion, forgetfulness, losing track of ideas, difficulty making links, difficulty staying focused, difficulty structuring thought, distortions in thinking, negative interpretations, discounting, false attribution of cause or effect, unrealistic expectations, inability to retain insights over time.

2 *On feeling*: emotional withdrawal, being uninvolved, distanced in relationships, not really there, unable to reconnect with feelings related to past events, suppressed anger, sadness or fear, what is said may lack emotional congruence, cut off, paradoxical over-excitement, aggressiveness, paradoxical exaggerated fears, depression, despair.

3 *On behaviour*: passivity with the counsellor, passivity outside the session, uncooperativeness, over-compliance, absences due to lateness, cancellations and missed appointments, denial of responsibility, disengaging from work relationships and social activities, seeming poor motivation, lack of fun/leisure pursuits, repetition in speech or behaviour, antisocial behaviour.

The effects a drug have on a person will vary with the particular drug, the dose, the length of time that it has been taken and the individual taking it. Counsellors can use information on the effects of drugs in Chapter 1 and their own and others' experiences to build up a sense of how much of the client's way of being is affected. No client displays all these signs and there may be other explanations such as physical or mental illness and the client's personality or circumstances.

However these are all aspects of the client that counsellors are well trained to observe and work with. What may help the counsellor to confirm that drugs are causing these effects are other signs from the client's body-language. The facial expression, pallor, eyes, hearing or speech may indicate drug effects. Sometimes a style of dress which seems to belong to a former time before the client took drugs or inappropriate responses suggesting a lack of connectedness, may raise the question in the counsellor's mind.

When drugs are helpful

ANTIPSYCHOTICS

Long-term medication may be essential for schizophrenic illness, because without it the client may lose touch with reality and become very distressed or be unable to function. This limits the depth of counselling, making exploratory work very slow, but the client can still use counselling to learn to cope with the illness and manage their lives.

LITHIUM

Long-term medication may be essential to control manic swings and the client may still be able to use counselling to explore past experience, coping with the illness and managing his life.

ANTIDEPRESSANTS

In severe depression when the client is dysfunctional, medication may help the depressed client to be accessible to counselling. The sedative effects can allow the client some relief from constant sleeplessness. The drugs can be gradually discontinued as therapeutic gains are made, thus making their use for a year unnecessary. By 'taking the edge off' the depression, they may limit accessibility.

Antidepressants are also used for shorter periods for bulimia nervosa and they may be helpful in some cases in breaking the cycle of vomiting and as an adjunct to counselling.

BENZODIAZEPINES

When clients are dependent, benzodiazepines must be continued until they have decided to withdraw, and be prescribed to allow the client to determine the pace of withdrawal. The drug withdrawal should always be integrated with counselling as drug withdrawal on its own does not deal with psychological issues. Benzodiazepines are sometimes used for short periods in alcohol withdrawal to prevent fits when their use should be closely monitored.

A single dose of a hypnotic benzodiazepine used occasionally may be helpful for people who are totally exhausted and unable to sleep. Benzodiazepines have other medical uses in hospital.

BETA-BLOCKERS

They are useful to control the physical symptoms of anxiety for example, when performers require a steady hand or until counselling can address the psychological issues.

When drugs are unhelpful

ANTIPSYCHOTICS

They are not appropriate for the treatment of anxiety and are likely to make things worse, nor can they be substituted for benzodiazepines in the belief that they are not addictive or may help withdrawal. Over-prescribing of more than one antipsychotic drug or with antidepressants and benzodiazepines gives no additional therapeutic benefit and adds complications for the counsellor in gaining therapeutic access. Repeated changes of drug may be tried in an attempt to control psychotic symptoms or reduce side-effects which might be better served by gaining the client's cooperation and compliance to the drug regime. Changes in prescribing without consultation with the counsellor may de-stabilize the counselling.

ANTIDEPRESSANTS

They may not be effective in mild or moderate depression and have no benefit used intermittently. They are used as a substitute for benzodiazepines, as a 'cure-all' for clients who really need advice, counselling or therapy.

BENZODIAZEPINES

Clients with a history of substance abuse or dependence are likely to become dependent both physically and psychologically. Clients with a history of physical or sexual abuse, eating disorders, traumatic experiences, pathological grief, will suppress the trauma and be unable to work on or resolve it. Conditions which are side-effects of benzodiazepines such as depression, agoraphobia, anxiety and panic attacks, may worsen. Benzodiazepines interfere with the grief process and should never be prescribed immediately following loss of any kind, at the time of funerals and during bereavement.

Psychosocial problems such as marital and relationship problems, financial difficulty, isolation, life transitions and over-working or 'stress', will remain undealt with. Benzodiazepines prevent clients engaging fully in counselling and the underlying issues being addressed.

GENERAL
Prescribing is usually unhelpful if it is used as a diagnostic tool for psychological problems. It is also inappropriate as a last resort, because the doctor does not know what else to do or simply because the client wants a prescription.

How the counselling is different

An understanding of medicine
When the client is taking prescribed drugs there are some things which are different for the counsellor. Some of the things which the counsellor learns in the process are also helpful if a drug-free client has been prescribed medication in the past. For example a client with an inhibited or protracted grief reaction may have been prescribed benzodiazepines immediately following the death, particularly if the death was traumatic, and understanding the part that the drugs played helps to make sense of the client's difficulty.

It is important to understand the medical model, the theories, assumptions and objectives which are inherent in it. Many studies which compare outcomes between medical and psychotherapeutic approaches fail to control for the direction of causality and measure outcomes which are objectives of medicine like symptom reduction or improved mood rather than self-efficacy or social functioning. The client has already become involved in understanding his problem in this way.

Since the client has already started treatment in one way, it is important to understand the doctor's clinical approach to diagnosis and treatment and to remember that these two stages are not necessarily separate nor approached in this order. Medical treatment of psychosocial problems is seen in terms of management and the doctor may not see any problem in the client having two separate sources of help. The implications of prescribing are that the client will have to return to the doctor regularly for repeat prescriptions and consultations.

While it is accepted practice not to start counselling a client who is still seeing another counsellor, no such understanding exists between doctors and counsellors. In fact there are recognized professional boundaries in medicine and it is probably helpful to fit into these procedures if they are compatible with the counsellor's practice. For example many counsellors ask their clients if they may make contact with the doctor who is prescribing to let the doctor know of their involvement. Doctors may not be aware of the dangers of splitting.

If the counsellor is not to find herself in a weak position professionally, having to defend her views, it is crucial that she has a good understanding of psychotropic drugs. First, she must know all the drugs the client is taking, what they are for, their effects both wanted and unwanted, how the drug should be taken and its limitations. Only with this information can the counsellor assess the effect on the client and the likely effect on the counselling.

Finding a balance between two approaches
Deciding on the appropriateness of the prescribing, and whether that is compatible with what the client is looking for in counselling, involves the counsellor in making judgements. Leaving the client to make all the decisions may still be possible but the client needs to know what is realistically possible. It is important that the counsellor is not pressured into accepting an impossible task since that is not in the best interests of the client.

Communicating these judgements to the doctor may involve challenging the doctor's opinion and treatment objectives, and combining challenge with tact is not always easy if the two parties have not communicated before. The more comfortable the counsellor is with the medical way of working, the more willing the doctor is likely to be to consider the problem from a different viewpoint. Respect for different traditions helps to promote agreement about an integrated approach in which prescribing is helpful and compatible with the level of counselling being offered.

Changes to the process
Allowing for the drug's effects on the client may mean that the counsellor has to assess at a very early stage what is missing in the interaction. The counselling relationship is going to be affected and the counsellor's sense of what is going on between them may require a different interpretation. The counsellor's feelings about engagement, rapport, accessibility and the nature of their attachment may mean that the counsellor is unduly pessimistic about working with the client. Reduced expectations of success will be communicated to the client who may lower his own.

There is no one method of counselling which works best with clients taking drugs. Probably only one way of working will prove insufficient. The client at different stages in his drug use will have very different needs. Finding what is effective at different stages may require that the counsellor modify or expand her therapeutic approach. It means following the client's progress very closely and adapting to it. So the counsellor needs to be very flexible, be prepared to experiment and learn from the client and take considered risks, sometimes getting things wrong and having to retrace steps.

Managing the process will be different because the counsellor is becoming an expert and for many this may be an uncomfortable idea. Worse is to come for the counsellor may be required to give information and advice. In fact one of the most frequent comments from clients is how secure they feel when the counsellor is willing to give clear factual information about drugs and accepts her responsibility for advising how the drugs are best used. Being willing to answer his questions and listen to his concerns about medication builds the client's confidence in his counsellor.

Given the limitations imposed by the drug use, the counsellor will need to make clear to the client that the drug use will probably be addressed before some of the problems that the client has brought. The counsellor needs the client's understanding and agreement for this if the work is not going to be constantly sabotaged. Including an educational component in the early stages will be familiar to counsellors who use cognitive behavioural therapy but less so to counsellors who use a more exploratory style. Conversely when the drugs have been withdrawn, much deeper methods are needed to access long-buried experiences.

Changes in the counsellor's style

The counsellor's personal style needs to be different too. In order to manage this complex process the counsellor is going to be more directive than is customary for many. Because of the drug effects on accessibility, the counsellor needs to be more intrusive in order to 'get in'. It may mean increasing the volume of the voice, varying the pitch and tone more, moving about in the chair and using broader gestures. Humour seems to be very important in this work and engages the client more firmly.

Because many psychoactive substances have a perceptual dulling effect, the counsellor needs to make allowances for the client's limited concentration span by giving short bursts of information or only making one point at a time. The work will involve a lot of repetition and the client may be reluctant to ask the counsellor for explanations to be repeated or expanded. The client may only be capable of small gains at a time but these need to be recognized.

Sedative effects which encourage passivity will slow the process further unless the counsellor is willing and able to generate much of the energy required. Counsellors who work with clients taking drugs need to be more active, sometimes dramatic, to make a point or access feelings. A counsellor who has the ability to act and be 'larger than life' without being excessive will be able to maintain attention and involvement on the part of the client. The client is not always able to do this for himself especially if he is depressed.

Being cut off in relationships may mean that the subtle nuances that the client is normally expected to pick up will be completely missed. This is especially true when inconsistencies become apparent to the counsellor. The client may not make the connection and need it pointed out. Confrontation may need to be done more obviously so that the client is fully aware of it. At the same time it must be combined with caring and respect so that the client does not feel diminished by it.

A very effective technique is the use of paradox, since it combines the two essential elements of confronting the inconsistency while acknowledging the need for it. By 'stroking the Child' (making a positive comment about the client), the counsellor removes the reason for the client's resistance to change – that is, gets around the defence. The discomfort with the inconsistency (cognitive dissonance) is not removed by blocking it out but by making the necessary shift. Examples of paradox:

> *Counsellor*: Well you have certainly given these drugs every chance to work [*stroke*], even though you say you don't notice much benefit.

The client may realize that he is not getting any benefit from the drugs and no longer has a reason to take them whereas a more direct challenge might be firmly resisted.

> *Counsellor*: I admire your frankness [*strokes courage*] in telling me you don't want to come off your drugs because you are afraid to.

The client thinks it might not be so bad.

The personal development of the counsellor
Counselling clients on drugs requires assertiveness in the counsellor who must be able to hold on to her own professional status when it is challenged and yet find understanding for the medical profession she is so often challenging. If the medical profession is more accepting of a counselling approach, the client may be resistant to having his drug use questioned or his request for counselling rejected.

This work is not for the raw beginner at counselling but every counsellor who sets out to do it must start from a position of relative ignorance. It requires a high level of competence and considerable experience to succeed and the counsellor may have to face failure and humiliation entering the medical world as a novice. There may be times when the counsellor is belittled for not knowing the generic names for drugs or even how to spell and pronounce them. It can sound foolish to have to ask.

Being willing to slaughter sacred cows means recognizing that the counsellor may attract some hostility and accepting this with dignity, especially when in a minority, can be painful. It is crucial that the counsellor gets informed supervision which goes beyond case supervision to include personal support. Having a medical consultant available who is not able to encompass the counselling issues too, is likely to be inadequate. Counselling supervisors who would consider themselves competent in this field are still rare.

Raising the issue
It might seem a lot simpler to forget about the drugs and leave all that to the doctors. Starting at the treatment stage assumes that if the client is on drugs then a diagnosis has been made and the drugs are correct or irrelevant. However a failure to challenge and get rid of the diagnosis in the client's mind will ultimately sabotage the counselling. The prescribing has been used to confirm the diagnosis and not seen as part of the overall problem.

A second reason to deal with the drug issue right at the beginning is that the client has a right and a need to know what is going to be involved in his counselling when the contract is agreed. If after several weeks of counselling the counsellor suddenly explains that she is unable to deal with the issues at depth because the client is taking drugs, the client may feel pressured to withdraw or give up, having invested a lot of time, effort and money which is wasted.

It may be tempting to 'Rescue' the client by not raising the issue of drugs (not confronting because the client is not strong enough to hear it) and the client is put into 'Victim' position. The switch may come when the client moves into 'Persecutor' announcing that he has not been helped and the counsellor is no good. Alternatively the counsellor feels frustrated at the lack of real progress and moves into 'Persecutor' announcing that the client is poorly motivated or difficult to help.

If the counsellor has a policy of not accepting clients taking drugs, it is important that this is stated early on, the reasons given and an offer made to refer elsewhere. This avoids the client telling his story, starting to engage with the counsellor or raising his expectations of help only to be rejected in a way that does not make it absolutely clear that it is for reasons of policy and not because of the client himself.

Conclusion

From a counselling perspective, working with people taking pre-scribed drugs means recognizing that two different models of psychological distress are involved and that the two do not always fit comfortably together. It means knowing when their objectives and approach are compatible and when they are not and being open with the client in sharing this perspective. Decisions are made by the counsellor about whether to accept the client, what the objectives can be and how to work with each client.

Assessment is a crucial stage which is easily omitted on the assumption that it has already been done by someone else. That first assessment or diagnosis has been done from a medical perspective and the counsellor needs to be aware of being over-influenced by it. Nobody else can ever assess a client for a counsellor because it is an assessment about entering a relationship together and the process is a mutual one with the client assessing the counsellor too.

Medication is sometimes necessary or helpful and the counsellor needs to understand and accept the limitations that continued drug use imposes. Sometimes the medication is unnecessary or unhelpful and can be withdrawn if the client chooses that option. Counselling during drug withdrawal and when people are off poses new and complex areas of work in counselling. There is no one way of working but it is possible to identify some of the principles by which the counsellor can be guided. These can then be incorporated into each counsellor's individual style.

3

Assessment and Setting Goals

Assessing for what?

Making an assessment is not an end in itself since it leads to some future action on the part of the assessor. Assessing a client, means discovering what brings him and how he sees his problem. In the usual way, the counsellor is estimating whether the person and the problem presented are within her realm of competence to understand and help. The counsellor is also making a judgement about whether she feels she wants to work with the client. If the drugs the client is taking are not mentioned or only indirectly referred to, it is easy to discount their significance for these judgements and omit them from the assessment.

The client is also making an assessment of the counsellor and her ability to understand the problem and throw new light on it, and the level of help the counsellor might offer. The client may believe that the drugs are not the concern of the counsellor since they are part of the existing treatment or because the client is looking for an alternative approach. Perhaps the client is wondering whether it is going to be profitable to work with this counsellor, and assessing whether the counsellor is a safe person to support him while counselling takes place. A counsellor who is unaware of the part the drugs are playing may inadvertently offer the client too little. On the other hand underestimating what may be involved may lead the counsellor to promise too much.

There are two things which are important about assessing clients on psychotropic drugs which may be less important with other clients. First, it is important for the counsellor to write down the client's answers preferably during the interview or immediately after. The verbatim replies often contain significant information that the client is not yet ready to deal with, and the written record keeps this available until much later so that it is not lost. The second point follows from this because writing down the client's answers in brief form means that the interview becomes semi-structured. This has the advantage that important issues are not overlooked and the interviewer keeps the focus and is not diverted.

This chapter takes the counsellor through the first contact made by the client, and describes how to assess the drug use and challenge the client to weigh up the advantages and disadvantages of drugs for psychological problems. Clients taking psychotropic drugs present situations which are particular to them, and can confront the counsellor unused to this field with special difficulties. The counsellor needs to assess what long- and short-term treatment objectives are realistic, what the client's and other people's expectations are and some sense of the likely outcome.

First contact

There are three ways in which clients come for counselling and these affect the first contact. A client may refer himself, arranging his own appointment, he may come as a result of somebody else's suggestion or 'nudge' or thirdly he may be sent. Self-referral is common in private practice, in some NHS centres such as community drug teams and in voluntary agencies. Here the client visits or telephones to discuss a problem in an informal way and the counsellor is working towards the client coming back to talk about the problem in more depth and face to face.

The client who comes at someone else's suggestion may be referred by a general practitioner to a practice counsellor, or by a tutor to a college counsellor, or by a manager to a personnel officer. The client who takes responsibility for making the first contact and appointment is more likely to attend that appointment than the client who has had the arrangements made on his behalf. Many counsellors in NHS settings have moved away from the medical practice of sending someone an appointment for this reason.

The client who is sent for counselling may be required to see his probation officer by a court order, may be allocated to a therapist by the consultant managing the team or may be given a key worker at a team meeting. This is not to suggest that the client does not approve of this but merely to point out that the client has had to make less effort himself and this may affect his commitment to counselling and therefore his ability to overcome the obstacles that he may face.

Increasing motivation

The counsellor needs to be looking for ambivalence about the referral not because it is a reason to reject the client but because it is inevitably there and is what the counsellor has to work with first. As Chapters 1 and 2 indicate, the client taking drugs has already had one solution which has worked so he must at some level be ambivalent about either his counselling or his drug use. This often shows itself when the client fails to turn up for appointments, comes late or forgets. Repeated cancellations and new appointments are indications of this but should not just be interpreted as lack of commitment to counselling since they are much more common among clients taking drugs than clients who are not.

Behaviour which reflects this ambivalence may show itself as erecting barriers to coming for counselling, such as not having the time, feeling unsafe on public transport, needing someone to come with them or being agoraphobic and asking for a home visit. It is important that the counsellor does not respond to these barriers with rigid statements about policy but gently and in a non-judgemental way accepts the difficulty while maintaining the view that the client can overcome these difficulties and that doing so is part of the therapy. It is equally tempting to do too much for the client and fit in with all the client's requests. Rather than going to see the client at home, a counsellor on the telephone might respond in another way. For example, after the counsellor has listened to the client's problem, and offered an initial appointment, the client responds:

> *Mavis*: I couldn't possibly come and see you. I can't go on buses because I have panic attacks.
> *Counsellor*: I can understand that would be frightening for you, but I'd like to talk more about it. Is there any way you could get here?
> *Mavis*: Well my husband can't bring me because he's at work.
> *Counsellor*: Is there anyone else? Or could someone come with you on the bus?
> *Mavis*: Well, a friend might, but I think when I got there I'd just panic.
> *Counsellor*: So you think if your friend came with you, you could come on the bus. Then we could talk about how we might help.
> *Mavis*: Well I suppose I could try . . .
> *Counsellor*: I think it may have something to do with your drugs so coming to see me might be the first step to overcoming your agoraphobia.

Sometimes what comes across in the first contact is the client's excessive neediness. This may be expressed through being in a crisis, needing an appointment urgently or being very demanding in other ways. Often clients like this are seen as manipulative because they have learned to conceal their neediness and ask for what they want in indirect ways. Unlike the client who is reluctant to come, they cannot wait and the counsellor is often aware that the client threatens to overwhelm her. Since these clients can be very difficult to contain counsellors may be tempted to reject them since that seems to be what is invited.

Bill: I don't suppose you can help me but I'm desperate.
Counsellor: It sounds as if you have tried everything without success.
Bill: I've got to get off these tablets but I can't do without them. I'm relying on you to get me off.
Counsellor: If you can't do without them, why are you trying to come off?
Bill: I am off them but the problem is I don't get a wink of sleep and its ruining my work. Can you give me something to make me sleep?
Counsellor: I think I would like to know more about how you came to be in this position, and the ways in which you have been dealing with not sleeping.
Bill: All I really want is to know what to do or a tablet or something.
Counsellor: Would you like to come and talk to me about it?

Counsellors who do not ask about their client's drug use right at the beginning of the first contact or in the assessment session are missing some important information that they need, to get an overall view of the client. Leaving the subject until the client raises it or until you have formed a good relationship, sounds reasonable but in fact the client may not be aware of its significance and may not raise it. Secondly drug use affects the relationship itself in ways that the counsellor must allow for right from the beginning. First impressions wrongly formed can be very hard to shift and even if the counsellor changes her perspective later, a pattern has been established.

A drug history is part of the overall picture of the client's past which the counsellor will be getting in an assessment session. This should include all medication since it will give a picture of illnesses in which psychological factors may have played a part. The psychotropic drugs should be identified by name, dose, how and for how long they were taken. This naturally leads the counsellor to ask about the reason for the first prescription, and what the client believed about his previous treatment and the use of drugs then. A less experienced counsellor can look up the drugs and discuss the implications with her supervisor later if necessary and this still allows time for the drug history to be taken into consideration.

The client's current drug use is very important because it is having an effect on the interaction between the counsellor and the client. Hearing that the client is taking antipsychotic drugs raises questions about whether the client has a psychotic illness which is being successfully controlled with drugs which probably need to be continued. If the client does not seem to fit this profile, the counsellor can begin to explore other possibilities such as the drugs being used in small doses for less serious psychological problems or even an inappropriate diagnosis.

A client using antidepressants may appear to be somewhat subdued or cut off, might be more anxious or even more depressed as a result of the drugs and it is important to distinguish between the client himself and the drug's effects on him. People taking antidepressants are less affected by them in their relationships with others so the counsellor should be able to reach the person and explore the problem unless the client is very profoundly depressed.

Benzodiazepines have a very marked effect on the assessment process and it is important for counsellors who pick up avoidance behaviour, emotional numbing, cognitive distortions and irrational beliefs, and who want to challenge the client's passivity, to be aware that much of this is just beyond the client's awareness. It is appropriate to raise it and to let the client know that much of what he feels is 'to do with me' is really to do with the effects of the drugs. These clients may have been 'written off' several times by professionals who put it down to the client being unhelpable rather than spotting the adverse effects of the drugs. A long psychiatric history should not deter the counsellor from making a contract but should alert her to the need to distinguish between the client and his previous 'help'.

Some effects on clients are difficult for the counsellor to respond to because of the underlying message or threat. However the counsellor chooses to respond, increasing the client's self-esteem and motivation are the primary objectives at this stage. Here are some possible responses.

Example The client says that all previous help has been rubbish and no use at all including the drugs. In spite of this he has been taking the drugs without questioning them for several years. The counsellor, sensing the suppressed anger, fears she is about to become the next helper to be rejected.

Response You sound very fed up that nothing anybody offers is any use to you. What do you think is the problem?

Example The client who is looking for an expert to solve all his problems including how to deal with the drugs. The counsellor is aware that she needs to use her expertise and give advice about withdrawing the drugs, but that when things become difficult this over-compliant person can blame her for failing.

Response I don't think I can tell you how to come off, but perhaps knowing about drug withdrawal you can learn how to manage it yourself.

Example The client rushes from one problem to another never finishing what he is saying. The counsellor cannot cope with the amount of material being disclosed and fails to pin the client down to anything in detail. The counsellor feels exhausted and out of control mirroring the client's experience of being out of control.

Response It sounds like you have a lot to tell me, so I wonder if we can take these one at a time in more detail and come back to the rest later.

Example The client defines herself very negatively as 'a born worrier', having 'bad nerves', 'can't cope' and resists all positive statements about herself. The counsellor is tempted to accept that they both know what a 'nervous breakdown' is without exploring what was happening at the time and making sense of it.

Response I'm not sure I know what you mean by a 'nervous breakdown', but I can see you feel pretty bad about yourself. What was happening to you then that felt so overwhelming?

Example The client appears to be in touch with very painful feelings and produces tears but this does not result in the expected relief. The counsellor may assume that previous losses have been resolved and be unable to understand the continued sense of distress.

Response I wonder if taking drugs has prevented you really finishing all your grieving, and you still have some painful feelings to come out.

Example A client who diminishes the importance of his drugs and says that they are a temporary crutch which he will dispense with when counselling is complete. Of course the work cannot be completed while drugs are still being taken.

Response I wonder if you realize your drugs might make it impossible to finish your counselling, and we might need to think about when would be the best time for you to come off.

Example A client who is 'all in the head' and wants to work everything out intellectually, ignoring what his body is telling him about his suppressed feelings. He may have many physical symptoms which he describes as an illness called 'stress'.

Response Perhaps your body is telling you something about feelings you have not really been in touch with.

Example A client whose need to take care of others over-rides her need to take care of herself. She may be unwilling to let go of over-nurturing others, seeing such behaviour as 'selfish'.

Response You are very good at taking care of other people. I wonder whether you could direct some of that into taking care of yourself a bit more right now.

Example The client who has idealized someone else, often a parent, with whom he is locked into a symbiotic relationship. The dependence is mirrored by the dependence on drugs. The counsellor risks attacking a 'perfect' relationship.

Response I wonder if you are a bit afraid of what separation might mean and the drugs were a way of dealing with that.

Exploring drug use

Exploring the reason for the original prescription, and what was hoped for from the continued use of the drugs, provides the opportunity to enquire what the client believes have been the drug's effects. Discovering whether the drugs worked at first, later and now, and what the long-term effects have been gets the subject of the drugs on to the agenda. The client may not have questioned his drug use in the past and find this a new direction in his thinking.

Some clients may have done a lot of thinking about their drugs and welcome the opportunity which the counsellor gives them to talk about them in great detail and at some depth. Many people have not felt free to question the prescriber about the drugs and it may be very reassuring to discover that the counsellor is prepared to give information and answer questions. Certainly long-term effects of drugs, both physical and psychological, need to be identified and made sense of. The client as well as the counsellor is separating the person from the drugs. This may represent an important change of focus.

Questions to ask clients

1 Name and dose of any drugs being taken.
2 How long have these drugs been taken?
3 How are the drugs being taken? Regularly or intermittently?
4 Has the client taken any drugs in the past?
5 What problems was the client having when the drugs were first prescribed?
6 Did taking the drugs help then? If so, how?
7 What did the doctor say about how the drugs should be used and for how long?
8 What does the client think the drugs do or are for?
9 Are the drugs still helping? If so, how?
10 Does the client still have the problem that he was prescribed for, or does he have different problems?
11 Has the client sought any other help where drugs might have been prescribed?
12 Has the client ever reduced or stopped taking his drugs? What happened?
13 What effects does the client notice the drugs have? Physical? Psychological?
14 Do the drugs affect the client's thinking, concentration or memory?
15 Do the drugs affect the client's ability to feel emotions or express them?
16 Do the drugs affect the client's behaviour or relationships with others?
17 What are the advantages of taking the drugs?
18 What are the disadvantages of taking the drugs?
19 Has the client informed the prescriber that he is seeking counselling? What did he say?
20 Has the client discussed his drug use with the prescriber recently? What did he or she say?

Challenging drug use

Using these questions in the assessment interview helps the counsellor get into a discussion of the issues, so that the part that drugs play in the overall problem begins to emerge. The counsellor is also beginning to get a sense of how much the client is dependent on drugs psychologically as well as physically and whether there will be resistance to a suggestion of drug withdrawal. Alternatively a picture of the client's reluctance to accept that drugs might have a part to play in the treatment may also come out. There are three main issues to explore.

Needing the drugs
Some people may need drugs because they are the best option or they may choose to continue taking them. Some examples of beliefs about needing drugs are:

Belief	Challenge
I need something to help me relax.	You have come to rely on something outside yourself to help you relax.
I can't sleep without tablets.	You slept without tablets once; you could do again.
I need to take one to get on a bus.	Actually you could get on a bus but you would feel frightened.
	Nobody really needs these drugs. (benzodiazepines)
They are for my nerves; they help me cope.	You can learn alternative ways to cope.
	Your nerves are fine; you are anxious about something.

Efficacy of drugs
People often have distorted ideas about the drugs' effects or the length of time they are effective. Some examples of this are:

Belief	Challenge
They must be doing me good, I can't manage without them.	These drugs are not a 'tonic'.
	Not being able to manage without a drug may mean you are dependent.
I know they still work; I calm down immediately.	None of these drugs acts immediately; that is what you believe.
Doctors wouldn't give them to you if they weren't safe.	These drugs are not as effective as some people believe.
I believe some people's brains don't have enough of a certain chemical so the drug restores the balance.	Benzodiazepines should only be prescribed for four weeks (maximum) and are not effective after four months.

Discounting the problems
One way to avoid the issue of the drugs is to diminish the disadvantages thereby making continuing seem the best option on balance. Some examples of this are:

Belief	*Challenge*
It would be too difficult to stop at my age.	It is not more difficult if you are older.
I doubt whether it is worth it.	Improving the quality of your life is always worth it.
I only take them occasionally.	When do you take them occasionally?
I know they don't really solve anything but I can't do anything else.	You might consider looking for a real solution.
Some people take them for years without harm.	That depends on how you think they may harm you.
My doctor says he takes them.	Your doctor is not you.

A treatment for symptoms

Drugs treat symptoms, not the underlying problem. Benzodiazepines are a treatment for the symptoms of anxiety and for insomnia, which is itself a symptom. The medical model only seeks to remove anxiety symptomatically and so the client needs to be pointed towards looking at what the anxiety is about if they have not already considered it. It is important however to make it quite clear that the anxiety itself cannot really be fully understood or dealt with until benzodiazepines have been withdrawn. Withdrawal of benzodiazepines itself may reduce the anxiety which is a long-term side-effect of the drugs.

In a similar way antidepressants are a treatment for the symptoms of depression which the medical model suggests may spontaneously remit. In some cases antidepressants may make the depression worse but if people are severely depressed they can have a useful and beneficial effect in making the client accessible to therapy. Gradually withdrawing antidepressants allows the symptoms to surface so that the feelings can be dealt with. Here symptomatic treatment is valid if it provides containment until the effects of therapy can be realized.

Beta-blockers are a good example of a treatment of symptoms only since they have no effect on the thoughts and feelings of anxiety but only on the physical symptoms. At some stage if real solutions are sought, the client is going to have to be willing to have his symptoms back again and manage them differently. It will be the symptom which lets the client know when he is being successful and finding an alternative way of dealing with his problem. Throughout the discussion with the client, a pattern of thinking will be emerging indicating to the counsellor where the client has reached in his awareness of the part played by his drugs. Whether the client is keen to be drug free or resistant to giving up drugs, comfortable with the knowledge that he needs them or reluctant to take them, the counsellor must start by acknowledging that drugs usually work as a treatment for symptoms, at least in the short term. The client needs to acknowledge this too, since a positive view of himself as a drug user preserves his self-esteem while he contemplates a view of himself as no longer taking drugs.

Advantages

1 Some (benzodiazepines and antipsychotics) are effective quickly.
2 They help people feel more in control.
3 They may help in a crisis while longer-term solutions are sought.
4 They relax people and make them sleep.
5 They may get people who are barely functioning started again.
6 They block off and numb bad feelings.
7 They calm down the worrying which makes the problem seem worse.
8 It gives time for the situation to change.
9 If there is no long-term solution, they make symptoms bearable.
10 They are easier, cheaper and less effort all round.
11 They are better than nothing, especially if no one knows what else to do.
12 They can preserve the peace if dealing with the problem would prove too costly in other ways.

Disadvantages

1 They are an external rather than internal locus of control.
2 They may discourage people from finding real solutions.
3 They do not re-activate natural sleeping patterns.
4 The symptoms may change or increase in number and severity.
5 The problem ignored may get worse.

6 People lose their good feelings as well as their bad ones.
7 They interfere with thinking, making problem-solving harder.
8 They are a means of avoidance.
9 They affect relationships, making people more cut off or aggressive.
10 They are a superficial solution and often make things harder and more expensive in the long run if special expertise is required.
11 Because they work, people can become dependent on them.
12 All drugs have unwanted as well as wanted effects.

In confronting the removal of symptoms with drugs, the counsellor must consider whether the client is willing to have the symptoms back again and take responsibility for finding an alternative solution. Removing the drugs and having the symptoms back implies that there will be a cost to pay before there can be any gain. It would be unrealistic on the part of the client, counsellor and prescriber to think that counselling is a no-cost alternative.

Secondly the symptoms are needed in the counselling because they make sense of and are the means of access to the underlying problem. It helps to feel anxious or depressed in order to work on discovering what the anxiety or depression is about. Exploring the content of the worrying that the client did during his sleepless night points to the underlying problem. Clients have to have their problem fully or 'be in touch with it' in order to work on it.

Case example
This is an example of raising the drug issue and discussing it with a client. Gloria started taking nitrazepam about three months after her mother's death, about 10 years ago. Her mother died of cancer and Gloria nursed her at home for about six months.

Counsellor: Did the drugs help?
Gloria: Oh yes! I couldn't sleep you see.
Counsellor: Do you think the problem sleeping had anything to do with mother's death?
Gloria: Yes, I think it had just hit me and of course I had to support Dad and I'd got my own family to think of.
Counsellor: What about you?
Gloria: What about me! I can see now it was too much especially after all those nights up with mother.
Counsellor: And since then you've changed to diazepam.
Gloria: Well after about two years I wasn't getting over it and the doctor thought I needed something to help me cope – I was weepy all the time – a real wet blanket you know.

Counsellor: What did you think you needed?

Gloria: Well my husband told me to pull myself together and throw the tablets away, so I thought I needed a kick up the backside and put them all down the loo.

Counsellor: What happened then?

Gloria: I fell apart and thought I was going, you know, mental.

Counsellor: You didn't realize that coming off like that was not OK, and that you were probably dependent on them?

Gloria: I thought only weak people depended on drugs so then I felt a real failure and thought I'd have to keep taking them all my life.

Counsellor: How do you think the drugs are helping you now?

Gloria: Well on the one hand I know I can't just stop just like that, but I would like to do without them and get back to normal.

Counsellor: Normal?

Gloria: Well have my feelings back – even if I have to have some bad ones too. It can't be right being the way I am.

Counsellor: How do you think the drugs have affected you?

Gloria: Well they make me tired all the time and I get bad headaches. But I've noticed I'm really quite tense and panicky when I have to do silly little things like go out for the day, even when I want to.

Counsellor: Do they affect how you are with people?

Gloria: Well I'm niggly with the kids but I suppose that's normal. But what's really silly is I'm planning my daughter's birthday party and I'm absolutely terrified – I can't even think about it. I know I shall have to call it all off at the last moment.

Counsellor: And you're still taking diazepam, so is it now part of the problem?

Gloria: Well you tell me!

Counsellor: I think it probably is. In fact you are coping with everything in your life as well as the unwanted effects of the drugs.

Gloria: I'm so glad you said that – I've been hoping you would.

Counsellor: So do you want some help to come off the drugs while we work on some of the other issues?

Gloria: Yes, I do.

Counsellor: I think that dealing with the feelings – perhaps about your mother's death – might have to wait until you are almost off, because the drugs prevent you doing that.

Gloria: I haven't grieved have I?

Counsellor: No I don't think you have.

Gloria, like many women, judged herself harshly as 'unable to cope' and had that view accepted and confirmed by the first prescription. The denial of her own grief and the responsibility she took for other people's feelings meant that anger at her loss was buried and the drugs were part of the way she did that. When the anger threatened to surface again, more drugs were added. The re-framing of her drug use as 'now part of the problem' is met with a rapid acceptance, as if she has been looking for someone to challenge that for her.

The counsellor sets up the expectation that counselling will address the drug use first and gives Gloria an explanation for that. This is important because she knows that grief work is on the agenda but cannot be tackled until she is almost off drugs. Without this agreement, clients may be impatient and sabotage the work and be constantly battling with the counsellor over who sets the agenda. There is a clear statement of insight into the underlying issue when she offers the counsellor her diagnosis, 'I haven't grieved have I?'

Case example

Mervyn had been taking a low dose of antipsychotic drugs for some months for severe depression and problems at work. When he came for counselling he was also taking an antidepressant.

Counsellor: What was the problem when you first went to see the doctor?

Mervyn: I was very anxious and I was under a lot of pressure at work.

Counsellor: And the doctor gave you fluanxol. Did that help?

Mervyn: Oh yes and when I went back four weeks later, he said to continue with them.

Counsellor: And then?

Mervyn: Well the next time I told him I seemed to be having problems at home, so the doctor doubled the dose and suggested some counselling.

Counsellor: What did you think about that?

Mervyn: I thought that if I could get over the tension, I would be alright and wouldn't need any counselling.

Counsellor: [*smiling*] That's only for if you get worse is it?

Mervyn: [*grins*] Yes, that's what I thought then.

Counsellor: What happened next?

Mervyn: Well next time I saw him, I was back to how I had been before and feeling very depressed – even thinking about ending it all.

Counsellor: What did the doctor think then?

Mervyn: He gave me some dothiepin as well to tide me over and said I really ought to come and see you to find out what it was all about.

Counsellor: Do you still feel as desperate as you did?

Mervyn: Yes, sometimes I do – especially last week – but I had a heart to heart with my wife and she thinks – well I know really – that its got a lot to do with my past.

. . .

Counsellor: What you've told me about your past makes a lot of sense of how you've been feeling recently. But if we are to work at that depth, I think we need to consider the best way to use your drugs.

Mervyn: OK. What do you suggest? Dr — said to just carry on 'till I saw you and then you would advise me.

Counsellor: I'd like to suggest that you think about coming off the fluanxol first because that might interfere with the counselling more, and continue with the dothiepin for now.

Mervyn: OK.

Counsellor: However we need to think about how and when you do it.

Mervyn: I'm going to see Dr — next week to tell him how I got on with you.

Counsellor: Why don't you talk to him about it and see what he says, and in the meantime, I'll write and let him know briefly what we've talked about and what I think about the drugs. How's that?

Mervyn: Fine. I'll do that.

At the start Mervyn had been inclined to see the drugs as the treatment, but the counsellor's gentle challenge about counselling being a last resort elicits an acknowledgement that he does accept that the counselling will treat what he knows is the underlying issue. It is this knowledge that he is going to get that deeper help that allows him to consider dispensing with the drugs. There is an acceptance that the drugs have performed a useful 'holding' function, and that they will continue to do so while counselling proceeds.

Mervyn's doctor has used prescribing sensitively and is very willing to integrate the two approaches. He has done the important motivational work and it is doubtful whether Mervyn would have considered counselling at all unless the doctor had proposed it. Clearly he is continuing to monitor progress and provide a place for Mervyn to discuss things especially his drug use. The trust the doctor expresses in the counsellor's judgement about the drug use, gives an important message to Mervyn about the doctor's expectations of the counsellor and therefore the counselling.

What may strike some counsellors as unusual about these examples is the willingness of the counsellor to give information about drugs and to make an evaluation of the part the drugs are playing. Expressing an opinion offers the client an important resource for accurate information and truthful judgement. The client needs to know that these will continue to be available throughout the drug withdrawal.

The second feature that is important is that there are no 'fudges' or mixed messages about whether or not drugs and counselling are compatible. Counsellors coming to this work for the first time might expect to experience a conflict between the two roles of counsellor and expert. However with practice the two can be integrated into a coherent and consistent style and this is necessary so that the client experiences the drug issues and counselling as integrated.

Case example
This is an example of negotiating a contract with a client to stay on drugs. Frank has been diagnosed as schizophrenic and is being maintained on antipsychotic drugs. Again the counsellor is required to set realistic objectives for the counselling work based on the preliminary assessment that Frank needs his drugs at least until a lot more work has been done. That opinion is offered quite clearly to Frank right at the beginning of their relationship.

> *Counsellor*: Well, Frank, you and I need to talk about what we are going to do together.
> *Frank*: You said we could talk about the drugs.
> *Counsellor*: I did, and I think you know I was concerned yesterday when you were talking about 'when you are off them'. What had you got in mind?
> *Frank*: I don't like the idea of taking them; they make me feel funny and 'not here' if you know what I mean.
> *Counsellor*: I guess they do, but what is the alternative?
> *Frank*: Do you think you could take me off?
> *Counsellor*: I could, but I'm not sure that you would be better off. What happened last time you tried to come off and manage without?
> *Frank*: Well I had a bad time and had to go back in (hospital), and they told me off.
> *Counsellor*: Realistically, Frank, I think you need to accept taking drugs at least for now as a way of keeping yourself safe, while we look at some of the other things you told me yesterday you want help with.
> *Frank*: You mean I've really got to take them?
> *Counsellor*: I think so. Perhaps that's the price of staying out of hospital. However I would like to hear more about how the drugs are affecting you and how you feel about yourself taking them. What else is important to you?
> *Frank*: Well part of coming to the hostel is to see if I can learn to handle money and shop and cook so that I can get a flat.
> *Counsellor*: OK. We are going to be working on that, but I guess that living here also means that there is a chance to take part in the group meetings and form relationships. What do you think your first target might be?

In this interview the counsellor has spotted that coming off drugs without alternative ways to cope was a way that Frank 'sabotaged' himself. Drugs and their effects on him are accepted as still on the agenda but the counsellor makes clear the view that using drugs is a way that Frank can be self-nurturing. This helps to support Frank's positive self-concept of himself as a drug user, while accepting that this is not a final decision and that Frank will have opportunities in the future to reconsider. Then the discussion moves on to explore other objectives such as developing social and living skills which can be done while he is still taking his drugs.

Case example

Sometimes the client knowing that the drugs are not a solution, decides that nevertheless they are her best option. Paradoxically the counsellor gives her permission to stay on, while leaving the door open for her to change her mind. Eileen is taking a benzodiazepine.

> *Eileen*:   I know that tranquillisers are not the best solution but I don't think I could come off. I've got used to having them. It would be too much hassle.
>
> *Counsellor*:   Perhaps it's difficult to think of giving them up if you can't see any real advantage.
>
> *Eileen*:   No, well Harry wouldn't like it you see. He likes me the way I am.
>
> *Counsellor*:   And Harry liking you is very important.
>
> *Eileen*:   You're right! I'm afraid of upsetting him and he's a bit suspicious of this counselling lark – I don't mean to be rude to you!
>
> *Counsellor*:   That's OK. It's important to take account of his views. Why don't you keep taking the drugs.
>
> *Eileen*:   And see how I get on with the counselling?
>
> *Counsellor*:   I'm afraid if you are taking benzodiazepines, then counselling can't go very far and certainly not into what you told me about your previous marriages.
>
> *Eileen*:   Then there's not much point is there? It's really all or nothing.
>
> *Counsellor*:   Not entirely, but perhaps now is not the right time. That leaves it open if you want to come back and talk about it again.
>
> *Eileen*:   Well I'm glad I can come back . . . and if anything happens to Harry . . . .

It would be very easy for the counsellor to accept Eileen's offer 'to see how I get on with the counselling' while she continues taking benzodiazepines. It might feel uncaring having listened to her story, to reject her for counselling in this way because she chooses to continue taking drugs. That would indicate a reluctance to say 'No' and set appropriate boundaries, and is a subtle form of 'Rescuing'. The outcome if the offer were accepted by the counsellor would be repeatedly working through the problems without resolution – 'no-exit' therapy.

Expectations of counselling

Asking about the previous help that the client may have sought gives the counsellor an opportunity to explore something of the client's expectations of the counselling he is now seeking. Especially the counsellor needs to know the focus of previous help, how it was given, how it ended and whether it is now perceived as a success or failure. Perhaps the help was successful then but that improvement was not maintained.

Was the previous help offered from within a medical framework or setting and did that affect the outcome? How long ago was the help offered and is the client's situation still the same or have events or the client moved on? Was the previous help too little, either in depth or time? Was the client offered too much then for which he was not ready? It is most important to discuss whether previous help is now seen as a failure on the part of the client or failure on the part of the therapy or therapist.

This will form the background against which the client is forming his expectations of the counselling being sought. If the client was taking drugs at the time he was last offered help and the drugs were ignored, and if the same kind of help is being offered the client may expect that what happened then may be repeated. It may be tempting to see drugs as a 'quick fix' or 'magic wand' but the client may implicitly be seeking a form of counselling which will perform the same function and avoid having to have painful feelings. One indicator of this is a client who is expecting the counsellor to be doing most of the work or working in non-intrusive ways.

Other people's expectations of the counselling will have an effect on the client's view. The doctor who has a positive view of counselling and sees it as a real solution and a far better alternative will raise the client's expectations. An unwillingness to take the risk of raising the client's hopes may indicate a fear of letting the client down on the part of the doctor who wants to protect the patient from disappointment. If the client has initiated counselling, the doctor who sees this as a positive step rather than a threat to the doctor's clinical competence, gives the client a large dose of encouragement and approval.

The client's family and partner can influence the expectations the client has of counselling. Have they already dumped all the family problems on the client and encouraging him to come for counselling further 'pathologizes' him? They might unconsciously be hoping that the counsellor will not succeed in understanding the client and they can then feel justified in not doing so. It might be difficult to express openly the hope that counselling will fail; a safer alternative might be lukewarm support.

If a partner realistically thinks that she and her relationship will form part of what is discussed, it would be unrealistic to expect her not to feel threatened by the counsellor in some way. A partner who can acknowledge her fears about the counselling disturbing the status quo helps the client to know that changes in relationships

Table 3.1 *What is therapeutically possible with clients on drugs*

Drugs	Therapeutic access	Approach to counselling	Level of working
Antipsychotics	Less	Prescriptive	Surface
Benzodiazepines	↑	↑	↑
Antidepressants	↓	↓	↓
Beta-blockers	More	Exploratory	Deep

will probably result from the counselling. A partner may offer to be included in the counselling although this is usually counter-productive. A better solution may be for the partner to get something for herself.

The counsellor has expectations about the efficacy of the counselling and much of this is conveyed by the way in which the client is accepted – freely or reluctantly. If counselling is offered freely, the counsellor must have a view or sense of how the client could realistically be in the future. Unless that view means improvement in the quality of the client's life, the counselling will be undermined. If reluctant acceptance is being offered that client will pick up a 'message': 'You have been allocated to me.'

Conveying to the client the expectation of success on the part of the counsellor is probably the most important message that is conveyed in the whole interview. The counsellor must make it clear that she is choosing to work with the client, and expects to succeed. Anything less will undermine the client's expectations too. It is the client's expectations which form one of the most significant predictors of the outcome. All through the counselling the coun-sellor will need to be aware of maintaining this for the client, because prescribing and drug-taking undermines it. As drugs are withdrawn, therapeutic access increases, counselling can become more exploratory and work can be done at greater depth. What is possible may vary with the particular drug, the dose and how long the drug has been taken, as well as for each individual person. Sometimes appearances are deceptive as clients may appear to be working on feelings by talking about or expressing them, but counsellors will notice that gains are not maintained between sessions. Lack of movement often indicates the blocking effects of the drugs.

Agreeing a contract for withdrawal

The first thing to agree is that the counsellor does not want the client to start reducing his drugs immediately. That would sabotage his success. It is sensible to assume both physical and psychological dependence and to ask the client to continue to take his drugs in a regular way but by the clock rather than by how he feels. This begins to break the psychological link. The contract for withdrawal should be a gradual one at the individual client's own pace, each step negotiated as they proceed. Speed is sabotage.

The client must make some preparations, such as reducing commitments, getting support of family and friends, arranging time off work for counselling or child care, talking to the doctor about the plan to withdraw. The third factor is to agree what the focus of counselling will be. If the client is on benzodiazepines, it will be on learning new skills or restarting old ones at first and dealing with the underlying problem will come later when the client is almost off. If the client is on antidepressants, the underlying issues may be accessible sooner. Fourthly the client needs to have some clear idea of his own objectives and the improved quality of life that he hopes for.

Choosing a therapeutic approach

Several factors influence the choice the counsellor makes about the way to start working with a particular client, and some parameters are fixed and some allow for flexibility. The setting imposes certain conditions but often these can be altered. Working in a medical setting may mean that all clients are assessed first by a consultant or general practitioner but that does not stop the counsellor doing her own. The policy of the organization may be that only individual therapy is offered, but if a case can be made for group work, the counsellor might have that option.

Limits are imposed by time, money or space, which might mean that the counsellor is only going to be doing part of what the client needs and referring on afterwards. Counsellors can come from many different backgrounds and that will affect their knowledge and skills. For some a medical background may help to give a sense of competence in dealing with drugs; for others it may impose constraints. Some counsellors will be limited by the styles of therapy they have been trained in: others may have developed a more eclectic approach.

Recognizing that all these factors can be changed or worked around in some way, it is worth thinking about the needs of the client taking prescribed drugs and the implications of the drug being used, in determining the approach chosen. It is when the counsellor works from this perspective that new or innovative ways of working are developed. It is also an opportunity for the counsellor to develop professionally by doing further training or study. The best time to learn something new is when you have a need and an application for it.

Different kinds of therapy may be exploratory or prescriptive (Rowe, 1991). Prescriptive models of counselling are more likely to focus on changing unwanted behaviour or thoughts. The prescribing of drugs means that behaviour, thinking and feelings are to be altered by pharmacological methods and so staying on or reducing drugs must use a behavioural approach. As well as changing drug-taking behaviour, counsellors are likely to be encouraging clients to attempt feared activities, engage in social activity, reduce over-working, learn and practice techniques such as relaxation and exercise programmes, make changes in diet or sleeping habits.

Talking is itself a changed behaviour for many clients whose drugs have limited what they have said or helped them not to say things. It is a means of expressing feelings and so disclosing, acknowledging and being vulnerable with another person have behavioural elements. In this way seeking counselling, coming to sessions as well as being in a counselling relationship, may be seen as significant behavioural changes. The counsellor's expectations are bringing about changes in behaviour and the positive reinforcement in the approval offered by the counsellor fits comfortably with good behavioural practice.

Often behavioural approaches are combined with cognitive therapies which aim to uncover and change irrational beliefs or negative distorted thinking. This may involve asking the client to reconsider whether those beliefs which were laid down in childhood are really so important now. They may be challenged by the counsellor as being harmful to the client in some way. The link between thinking and feelings may offer the client a way to change how they feel by changing how they think, through such means as reality testing, thought stopping, changing negative thoughts or visualization.

As clients are ready to go deeper and work on the underlying issues, exploratory models of counselling lend themselves more to this stage. Psychodynamic or analytic styles of working seek to help the client to understand his present experience in the light of his past, and particularly formative years. They use what occurs in the relationship between the counsellor and client to promote insight into the effects that the client's past still continues to have. Person-centred counselling makes particular use of the quality of the therapeutic alliance between counsellor and client, with the counsellor giving the client important feedback about the way the counsellor is experiencing him.

Personal contruct therapy is essentially exploratory although it is in some way cognitively focused. What is important in choosing an approach for clients on drugs, is to remember the depth at which a particular approach works. In the same way existential counselling requires greater depth for the exploration of feelings and for the client to be able to search for a sense of his own being. Transactional Analysis seems to be fairly accessible to clients on drugs when structural and transactional analysis link present experience with Parental messages in infancy. Later exploring the 'script' and 'games' can promote working at greater depth.

Clients who have been taking drugs, especially if they have taken them for many years, have often 'forgotten' ways of being and interacting with others that have to be re-learned. If drugs have been used to supplement naturally occurring chemicals which are then less effective, naturally learned living skills and ways of coping with life will have become extinguished through lack of use. Clients will need an educational element in their counselling at first to teach them the effects the drug has had on them and to identify what they no longer do for themselves automatically.

Personal interactional skills can be learned during the process of counselling but attention to areas such as awareness of off-putting mannerisms, aggressive body-language, lack of turn-taking in conversation, indirectness in making requests and breaches of boundaries are often better tackled directly in an educational style. Many clients on drugs will benefit from learning to be more assertive and find that these social skills increase their self-efficacy, a significant marker of progress.

The choice of individual counselling means that the client can have the undivided attention of the counsellor and this one-to-one relationship provides a more intense experience. The treatment goals can be specifically tailored to the client and in many ways the client can progress faster, working on what is most important to him. It provides a setting in which the counsellor can be more flexible, moving between dealing with the drug issues and the underlying problem as it emerges and as the client is ready. Since clients on drugs often discover past physical and sexual abuse or have sexual problems as a result of drug use, individual therapy may be the first choice if the counsellor has an inkling of this at the outset.

Groups have a very important part to play in counselling clients on drugs because they offer the client more than a single counsellor can. There is the experience of not being alone with the problem and the opportunity to form more than one relationship. It is easier to reject what is offered by the counsellor than what a fellow group member says. Often clients will raise issues that might otherwise have been avoided or suppressed by others in the group. There is a greatly increased opportunity for social interaction and the group provides an ideal setting for educational and skill training sessions. Above all most people who are hesitant at first come to value the support they receive for making changes.

The third main choice for the counsellor is whether she will take sole responsibility for the client or use a 'shared care' approach. The most usual instance of this is where the prescribing is done by one person and the counselling by another. It is important that there is some agreement between the two about boundaries and particularly who will advise the client if drugs are being withdrawn. There may also need to be some agreement for liaison so that the counsellor can ask the prescriber to change a drug or prescribe a new one.

A different problem arises where the counselling itself is to be shared. This may be the case where drug withdrawal is done by one counsellor and deeper therapy aimed at the underlying issues is done by another. The two cannot usually proceed at the same time and it is better if there is an agreement that the drugs will be dealt with first and that relationship ended before the client moves on. Some clients will be seeing a community psychiatric nurse for injections, perhaps a social worker for individual work and attending a self-help group or voluntary agency. Clear boundary setting which includes the client will help to avoid conflict.

An integrated approach where at least all the counselling is done by one counsellor, avoids the problem of splitting the counsellors into good and bad, and giving conflicting messages. Many prescribers will willingly cooperate if they are assured that sound advice is being given. However this requires a high level of expertise in many areas for the counsellor and might be an approach which is developed gradually by less experienced counsellors, after additional training. It is important that the counsellor knows that clients on drugs can be very hard to reach and emotionally demanding if sole care is undertaken, particularly in individual counselling in private practice.

The counsellor has therefore three main choices to make. First, to decide on the approach to be used. All clients will need some educational or skill work ranging from a very intensive package if they are taking antipsychotic drugs, less if taking benzodiazepines and at least information about their drugs and withdrawal if they are taking antidepressants. Assertiveness skills are often necessary too. The approach is then more prescriptive while the drug withdrawal proceeds and changes in thinking and behaviour are addressed. Finally the exploratory work can be done, and should not be omitted when clients are off drugs. They had a reason for taking drugs in the first place.

The second choice is between individual and group therapy. Here the decision should not be left to depend on time, money or availability of premises. All of those can be changed as can the training, experience and preference of the counsellor. What should take priority is what best meets the needs of the client if at all possible. Where the choice is limited as for example in private practice, counsellors should try to exploit the advantages of individual counselling and diminish the disadvantages. Sometimes if the counsellor is only doing part of what is needed, a referral elsewhere may offer what has not been available.

The last choice is between shared care and an integrated approach. If the client has a great many needs it may be more appropriate for care to be shared between several workers and several agencies, who each provide their specialist area. Often responsibility is shared with the prescriber. If the policy of the counsellor's employing agency permits and the counsellor's knowledge and skill are sufficient, then an integrated approach means that the client is maintaining one therapeutic relationship, all issues are addressed in turn and there is less likelihood that part is missed.

Conclusion

The quality of any counselling depends in no small way on the quality of the assessment. It is by reviewing the outcome of the counselling that the counsellor can see the relevance of what came out in the first interview. This is especially true where issues not addressed at the beginning such as the drug use, can rebound on the counsellor because it may then be too late to go back and rectify the mistake. Fortunately experience is a good teacher as long as the counsellor is prepared to see the implications of what she did or failed to do.

At the end of the assessment the counsellor and client will have agreed whether the client is going to continue with his drugs or withdraw from them. They will have agreed how and when the withdrawal will take place and whether that will be included in the counselling or done elsewhere first. Secondly they will know what their mutual objectives are and that these are realistic and achievable. It is implicit that the client expects an improved quality of life as a result of coming off drugs even if at first he will experience a loss.

Finally they will have some idea of when the underlying issues will be addressed and the counselling can proceed at depth. There will nevertheless be room for some of these later objectives to be changed as the client becomes more aware of the real problem or as unknown experiences and difficulties emerge. The assessment leads to treatment and the next question must be where to begin.

4

Drug Withdrawal and Learning Alternatives

This chapter describes the process of integrating drug withdrawal with counselling. At this stage the client needs a structured approach which moves him on because of the tendency while on drugs to get 'stuck' and keep re-working the same material. It is fairly interventionist because the client on drugs seems to need that. The counsellor has to work to keep the client engaged, and respectful but firm confrontation mixed with humour keeps up the energy level of the sessions.

The chapter covers the setting of boundaries both for the counselling and for the drug issues. The symptoms are explored and understood, defining what will be addressed in the counselling at a later stage. Before drugs are withdrawn the client has to find and agree to use alternative ways to cope with stress, anxiety, the return of difficult feelings as well as withdrawal symptoms. Distorted thinking, low self-esteem and understanding oneself come next, followed by the client being invited to make some significant changes in the way he lives his life. Finally but most importantly, 'sabotage' and relapse to drug-taking are dealt with.

Clients who are taking antipsychotics or benzodiazepines will need to start here, while clients taking antidepressants may not need all that this chapter contains. Alternatively, because clients taking antidepressants can sometimes work at greater depth, much of this material can be integrated for them with more exploratory approaches, and used whenever seems appropriate. The section on drug withdrawal will need to be used perhaps weekly or fortnightly to check progress and negotiate further reductions. It fits well at the beginning of the session, but if clients are too focused on their withdrawal symptoms, it can be left until the end so that other issues are not squeezed out.

Boundary setting

In order to help the client re-establish control in his life, the counsellor needs to reach an agreement about how and when the drugs are going to be taken. If the client has been following instructions about taking his drugs, it is still important that he understands the reasons for this. Unless he takes control of his drug use while he is still taking them, he will not be able to take control and stay off. This means teaching the client about the drugs, and follows on from what was started during the assessment stage.

All drugs have side-effects for they would not be produced and taken if they did not. Some effects are wanted and some are unwanted and the unwanted ones are what are referred to as side-effects. The client is taking them for the wanted effects and needs to know what these effects are, because alternative ways of achieving the same effect have to be found, if the drugs are going to be stopped. If the client is going to stay on drugs, even temporarily, the drug's usefulness to him will help him to keep taking his medication willingly and consistently.

Unwanted effects can sometimes be alleviated by taking a slightly lower dose, but the dose cannot always be changed easily since for example, reducing a benzodiazepine requires planning because it may produce a withdrawal reaction. A client who knows that the unwanted effects will disappear when the drug is stopped may be motivated by that to consider withdrawal; it will be a gain. If the drugs must be continued, understanding that unwanted effects are probably inevitable may help a client to accept these effects and find ways to make them more bearable.

There is usually a preferred way to take drugs and clients need to know what this is and the reason for it. It makes sense to take a single dose of a sedative at night before sleeping, and to take more stimulating drugs in the morning. Drugs which have a shorter half-life such as lorazepam are best taken at regular intervals during the day so that the effect is kept more or less constant. This helps to avoid the problem of experiencing a withdrawal effect between doses even when the drug is not being reduced.

Chaotic use, such as taking in response to feared tasks or situations, delaying as long as possible before taking a dose, increasing and then decreasing the dose, missing some doses out altogether, leads to increased discomfort and prevents people getting the best benefit. For example if clients are starting anti-depressants, taking regularly and increasing gradually helps to reduce unwanted effects as tolerance develops.

If the client has decided to come off drugs, he needs to know why he should continue with them for a while. The reasons might be because he is dependent, needs time to plan for withdrawal, has learnt about withdrawal before he reduces, and wants to start from feeling confident. Stabilizing the drug use allows the client to feel comfortable and confident before he starts. It also deals with the psychological dependence which taking 'as and when necessary' sets up. The boundary should be: 'Take the same amount, at the same time every day, regardless of how you feel.'

It is important, particularly with benzodiazepines, to stress the effects that the client is not getting. After four months' continuous use of anxiolytics and 14 nights' continuous use of hypnotics, there are few if any benefits. The client, not the drug, is coping with his life. Antidepressants are continued because they help to make the client accessible for counselling not because they treat depression. The client still has to understand the reason for a depressed mood. Antipsychotic drugs are continued because they control the unacceptable symptoms of psychosis. Nobody really knows very much about predicting if and when psychotic illness can be cured.

At the same time the counselling needs to focus on new boundaries for daily living so that a regularity and stability is established. It is important to explore what has happened to rising and sleeping times, and whether the client is sleeping at other times. The eating pattern may have been lost and a daily discipline about taking meals at regular times including breakfast should be started. One of the indications of severe depression is the unwillingness to get up in the morning and loss of interest in eating so setting a pattern is crucial in changing this.

Clients on benzodiazepines and antidepressants may have become inactive so purposeful activity such as exercise for relaxation and interest, social contact, relief of boredom, or work reduce passivity and give the client purpose when he can generate little from inside. It is also part of increasing the sense of competence for the client to be taking active steps to make himself feel better. None of this is 'done to' the client; it is all 'done by' the client, and moves the locus of control from external to internal.

Case example

Arthur had been taking sleeping tablets of various kinds for over 25 years, with a year or two off from time to time, but for most of the time for the last six years. His doctor had let him change drugs when the current one seemed to have lost its effect, and he had actually built up quite a stockpile. He was trying to come off and had been trying for a long time with little success because when things became unbearable he increased his dose. He had no idea how he could manage without sleeping tablets and saw insomnia as a chronic illness.

When the counsellor explored how the drugs were being used, it emerged that he waited until about 2 a.m. before he took one and if he managed to fall asleep he missed it out altogether. Sometimes he would miss out the drugs for several nights and struggle with broken sleep often waking feeling tired and exhausted. He stayed in bed until about 11 a.m. and sometimes took a nap during the afternoon if he felt like it. On those days he would stay up later and not go to bed until 1.30 a.m. so effectively his day-time had moved later and later.

Breakfast was completely missed because he was in bed trying to get back to sleep or he was asleep. Feeling exhausted all the time he took little exercise and as he had got older, the less he did the less he felt capable of. Before lunch he was at his most crotchety and so he had agreed with his wife that she would get on with her life and leave him alone until afternoon. She went out to visit friends so he had few opportunities to meet people. He enjoyed a couple of drinks in the evening, one of the few pleasures left, but although they helped him feel relaxed while watching television, they probably made sleeping more difficult not easier.

Life had been reduced at all levels and even the tasks of daily living seemed enormous. Tackling bills and minor maintenance jobs felt like an effort and more and more things built up with which he felt too tired to cope. Arthur was in a downward spiral where his inactivity increased his problems and his problems seemed to paralyse him. He also believed he needed much stronger sleeping tablets because 'if I could only get a decent night's sleep, I would be able to cope . . .'. This kind of belief is very seductive to the client, prescriber and counsellor.

The boundaries were set like this:

1 Take only temazepam 20 mg, every night, to stabilize.
2 Keep a record of times when all tablets are taken, including analgesics.
3 Move bed-time back to 11 p.m. in two steps.
4 Get out of bed every day at 7.30 a.m.
5 Wash, shave and dress and eat breakfast before 9 a.m.
6 Do not sleep during the day.
7 Take two periods of exercise per day, i.e. walk to post a letter.
8 Find something to do and somebody to talk to each day.
9 Avoid alcohol during the evening and reduce the quantity.

Arthur undertook to do this and was very pleased with his success especially when he discovered that he felt less tired and had started to sleep better. Moving the client from passivity to activity is especially important if he is very depressed, and gives him a different experience of himself. What Arthur could not have known was that by using his hypnotics in the best way, he actually felt better before he started to come off, and he had stopped the self-defeating cycle of not sleeping and feeling tired. He himself volunteered the thought that alcohol was probably making things worse and he could leave it off for a while.

Boundary setting around the counselling can be done in many different ways and each counsellor will have her own style. There is usually an agreement to come regularly and for a set amount of time, and what the agenda will be and how the counselling will proceed. Clients dependent on a substance often have a problem about dependence on people too. Some counsellors deal with this by being very firm that no access to the counsellor or anyone else in the agency is allowed outside the session. Some counsellors work more flexibly letting the client learn through feedback how to establish his own internal boundaries.

The client who is planning to withdraw from drugs may need extra help and support during the withdrawal either by agreeing to extra sessions, or by telephone contact or by dropping in to a centre or self-help group. Awareness of this is important at the beginning so that at least during drug withdrawal or if the client feels suicidal, both know what they have agreed. This prevents the client having to go elsewhere for help, taking more drugs, or going to his doctor with the problem. Counsellors who have very well-established internal boundaries rather than relying on external rules usually find they can cope better with the demand for flexibility. It can be very hard to get it right all the time with some clients.

Making sense of the symptoms

Exploring with the client the context within which he lives his life begins the process of making the symptoms understandable and therefore reassuring the client that he makes sense. The first clue may lie in how he spends his time working inside or outside the home. Is it stimulating or boring, too much or too little, brings or lacks recognition? Does the person exercise control over his working environment or is he tightly controlled and is that how he would prefer it to be? Does he work with others or alone and would he prefer it to be different?

Threats to the client's sense of security can come from a realization that he has already reached his career peak and is on the way down or even that he is never going to get started. Anxiety may be about the threat of redundancy and loss of income or about his relationships at work. Fears about competence are often described as poor self-confidence and a client may not have a sense that he is good enough. The workplace can be an abusive environment with autocratic management styles and subversive undercurrents being disguised so that the client cannot pin-point what his feelings are about.

Relationships in the household as well as the wider family can be part of the problem too. Exploring the dynamics of the current family as well as the family of origin can identify the role that the person has adopted in relation to others. Where does the power reside and how is that power base maintained? What are the family's beliefs about age and gender and how is the client's behaviour encouraged or proscribed? What do the members of this family keep hidden from themselves and how is conflict managed?

Clients who have symptoms of anxiety or depression always have unrecognized losses, either anticipated or defended against. Talking about the client's personal relationships may identify whether close relationships are deep or superficial. Which significant people has the client lost and how have these been mourned? Have there been significant others who have been emotionally unavailable and therefore made attachment difficult? Does the person now form 'clingy' or 'self-sufficient' relationships prolonging the sense of loss?

In some way, factors in the client's life produced a climax of symptoms that led him to seek medical help and it is particularly important to explore the two years before the first prescription to see what produced that climax. The symptoms were 'trying to provoke' the client to make some necessary changes in his life. The need for these changes was ignored and the drugs were used to remove the symptoms and avoid making changes. Some clients may have recognized the need to make changes, but felt it was a high price to pay and that drugs were an easier option.

Through investigating what has happened to the client since that first prescription, the counsellor may see the evidence of how changes were ignored and everything was returned to 'normal'. This removal of the symptoms while ignoring what they were about, needs to be shown to the client, partly to undermine the belief in his own 'illness' and partly because the client needs to recognize that some changes will need to be made before reducing the drugs. Removing drugs without other changes will merely expose the client to an increase in symptoms. Previously that may have been defined as 'evidence of the underlying illness' and the counsellor must re-frame it.

Case example

Roger has been taking benzodiazepines for insomnia and panic attacks for two years. He works as an engineering technician and has been with his company for 15 years. Recently new working arrangements have meant travelling to another company site two or three times a week and Roger now has to make presentations on projects. He had very little post-16 education and worries about his poor grasp of language which he fears will 'give him away'. His parents died suddenly three years ago and he misses his mother who was the dominant one. His wife is a 'home-lover' but has a part-time job in a shop and they do not go out much.

Roger leaves for work early if he has to travel and gets home late, bringing the data for his reports to work on in the evenings. He tries to catch up on sleep at the weekends and spends Sunday going over and over the presentations trying to get them word-perfect. The first panic attack occurred in the car and he now dreads journeys and is having obsessive thoughts about car crashes. He has worked out a way of coping by always avoiding motorways. His doctor thought about giving him antidepressants for the panic but suggested he try counselling first.

Roger's life is totally dominated by work although he does not fit the stereotype 'workaholic' label. He has also accepted several medical diagnoses and makes few connections between symptoms and suppressed feelings. First he needs a boundary around the time devoted to work which displaces other aspects of his life. The second task is to make sense of the symptoms which is the way his body complains psychologically. Thirdly the avoidance shows the way in which he deals with internal discomfort by externalizing it.

This phase of the counselling has a clear educational focus because the concepts of anxiety, depression, panic, obsessions, stress and so on must be understood from a psychological perspective. The place of symptoms as the external expression of emotional distress and an understanding of the physiological process of arousal reduces the sense of being out of control which many clients find so frightening. Myths about the importance of sleep established perhaps in childhood, can increase anxiety since many people believe that the amount of time they sleep should be under their control.

At this stage learning to control physiological arousal through relaxation techniques such as slower breathing, self-hypnosis, tensing and relaxing muscles, restores control to the client. Developing a better sleep routine, taking regular exercise and eating proper meals are important changes that help a client have alternative ways to cope before he makes any changes in his drug use. It also gives the client an experience that making life-style changes is what he should have done in the first place. The more difficult changes will come later but this is where the client gains much confidence.

Alternative ways to cope

1 Make a change in life-style: reduce work, responsibility, or reduce expenditure; take stock.
2 Express feelings: identify suppressed feelings; talk about fear, guilt and anger.
3 Tackle the problem: confront the real problem; do not avoid doing difficult things.
4 Get advice: learn new skills; ask for help when needed; get expert information on money, property etc.
5 Accept the way you are: recognize real failings and past mistakes and real strengths too.
6 Learn to relax: switch off sometimes and take a break; take exercise, wind down at the end of the day.
7 Increase leisure activities: have fun; be more active in leisure time.
8 Make time for self: for eating, resting and exercise; time without responsibility to or for others.

Counsellors can encourage people to take a long-term view of themselves and their problems, thinking how they were, what they did before drugs and how they would like to be in the future. It helps to remind people that this is the only life they are going to get; it is not the dress rehearsal. This helps people to focus on determining priorities and may shift the balance from focusing on symptoms or trivial events in their lives to the main issue of discovering a more satisfying way of living their lives.

Managing the withdrawal

One of the most important ways to reduce anxiety is to make the unknown known. However much the client fears what may happen if drugs are reduced, knowing what to expect immediately makes the fear more manageable, and hence reduces it because he is less afraid of the fear. Therefore it is important to start by giving the client accurate information about withdrawal effects, an opportunity to discuss and ask questions, and support to plan how best to cope if they occur.

Sometimes a client will have made previous attempts to reduce or stop taking drugs and may have had some time drug-free before starting again. This provides the counsellor with a chance to explore the client's expectations of how he will be this time, and possibly a warning that what was seen as evidence of failure needs to be re-framed as useful learning experience. The client may also need the reassurance that this time he will be in control of withdrawal.

Part of the client's expectation is that he will return to the way he was just before he started drugs, and this belief should be challenged by the reminder that he is not the same person in the same situation as he was then. Secondly he is having counselling to deal with the problem and he now realizes what his problems were about. The fear about falling apart if drugs are reduced may have been reinforced by a previous attempt at withdrawal which was done too quickly. The client may have assumed 'it must be me' rather than realizing that the symptoms were a severe withdrawal reaction.

Previous withdrawal attempts

1 If the person did have a bad experience, what went wrong?
2 Was he sufficiently informed about drug withdrawal and had he made the necessary preparations?
3 Did the client really choose to reduce, and who was in charge of the withdrawal?
4 Did he know what was happening and was there anyone to ask?
5 If he found he could not cope, did he have any alternatives in place first?
6 Did he do too much too quickly and sabotage himself?

The client who has already had a successful experience of reducing will be more prepared to repeat that success if he understands what was right about it. It may have broken the link between himself and the belief that he 'needs' drugs. Perhaps he can see he has made progress since then by seeking counselling and starting to work on his problems in new ways. He has also learned some useful strategies about drug withdrawal which he can repeat each time until he is off. It is still important for the counsellor to monitor progress because each response to reduction may not be exactly the same.

Other people's reactions to the client's previous attempts to reduce drugs can indicate 'hidden agendas'. The doctor, partner, family and friends may have been encouraging, supportive, sympathetic or understanding. On the other hand they may have sabotaged, been dismissive, not wanted to know or responded with 'I told you so'. Was the client's own helplessness and panic mirrored by those around him? How much does the client rely on other people's views of things and how much is he able to decide for himself his own reality?

Principles of withdrawal

1   People go at their own pace with no pressure.
2   Stabilize drug use and develop alternatives.
3   Make a small and manageable reduction and wait at least two weeks.
4   If a withdrawal reaction occurs, do not increase dose again.
5   Cope with the withdrawal symptoms in non-drug ways.
6   Deal with feelings which emerge as far as possible.
7   When people are comfortable and confident, reduce again.
8   The counselling addresses skills lost while on drugs.

During this process, clients may find it useful to record a daily drug diary, which should include alcohol, tobacco and analgesics and the times they were taken. Keeping a record of withdrawal symptoms helps client and counsellor track the progress of adjustment to a lower dose. When memory is unreliable, a drug diary may increase the client's sense of control over symptoms and demonstrate that the symptoms do go away as the withdrawal syndrome subsides.

Example of benzodiazepine withdrawal

Reductions should be proportional not absolute values. That is they should be appoximately an eighth of the total daily dose rather than a set number of milligrams, as far as possible. This seems to be the rate people can comfortably tolerate. For example, 20 mg, diazepam could be reduced like this: 20mg → 18mg → 16mg → 14mg → 12mg → 10mg → 9mg → 8mg → 7mg → 6mg → 5mg → 4mg → 3mg → 2mg → 1.5mg → 1mg → 0.5mg → off.
2.5mg lorazepam could be reduced like this: 2.5mg → 2.25mg → 2mg → 1.75mg → 1.5mg → 1.25mg → 1mg → 0.75mg → 0.5mg → 0.25mg → off.

Counselling could be weekly for 8–10 weeks while the client learns how to manage the withdrawal, with extra contact for advice if necessary. Counselling may then be spaced out with minimal support for a while until the client is nearly off. Feelings start to become accessible at around 2mg diazepam, but some clients cannot work at depth until they have been abstinent for a while. People reducing 2.5mg lorazepam (which is actually equivalent to more than 20mg diazepam) do not complete the withdrawal more quickly because they probably need to space out their reductions more.

There is no set time for withdrawal because each person goes at the pace with which he is comfortable, and if he is reluctant to reduce when he has adjusted again, the counsellor should explore the resistance and deal with it rather than over-riding the client. It is not unreasonable to assume that the client will need four weeks or more between reductions and longer if necessary. Hence two years to complete drug withdrawal is not exceptional. Speeding it up makes the symptoms worse, more numerous and produces the more serious symptoms, and does not allow time for psychological adjustment.

Example of antidepressant withdrawal

Greater proportional reductions can be made for antidepressants but the length of time between reductions although shorter should still be at a pace the client chooses. 75mg dothiepin could be reduced like this: 75mg → 50mg → 25mg → off.
30mg clomipramine could be reduced like this: 30mg → 20mg → 10mg → off.

If the first reduction seems too much, half-dose reductions can be used for people particularly sensitive to withdrawal effects. However counsellors should consider whether the difficulty is primarily due to pharmacological or psychological adjustment.

Thinking and self-esteem

The way the client thinks about himself, other people and the world affects how he feels. People who are anxious or depressed feel fear, sadness and anger, and often have a very distorted view of themselves and the world. In addition benzodiazepines and anti-depressants can increase both anxiety and depression and contribute to this style of thinking as well as being psychologically undermining in themselves.

One of the ways the counsellor can access her client's thinking is to ask him how he was thinking about himself before he reduced his drugs and what his expectations were. When the client is about to make a change in his behaviour or do something difficult that has previously been avoided, does he notice what he is thinking at that moment? Ask him what thoughts he has if he imagines setting limits on other people's demands or asking another person for help or support.

In relation to drugs, you might hear:

'I'll try but I'm terrified.'
'I couldn't manage without them.'
'I'm really ill, I need drugs.'
'I shouldn't go against my doctor.'
'I might go mad or crazy.'

'I'll fall apart.'
'I'll probably have to go back on them again.'

In relation to making changes, you might hear:

'If I go on the bus, I'll have a panic attack.'
'I just can't do it, everything will go wrong.'
'I'll never be like other people.'
'I doubt whether I have it in me.'
'It might make things worse.'
'No matter how hard I try, I can't get it right.'
'I can't do anything until I've finished all my work.'

In relation to other people, you might hear:

'You have to work overtime – everyone does.'
'It would be selfish not to help out.'
'If I said No, they wouldn't like me.'
'I'm not really a very nice person.'
'They must think I'm a real wimp.'
'They would get angry with me.'
'I'm scared to trust anyone.'

All of these statements and many similar ones contain a distortion of reality or a discount of the person himself. Rather than teaching a course in anxiety management, the counsellor can challenge the truth of these statements as the client expresses them. This means that the counsellor is using what the client offers and is working directly with that. Encourage the client to recognize how thinking in this distorted way makes him feel.

The counsellor can challenge by reflecting back the distortion so that the client recognizes it and modifies it to a more realistic statement. The right intonation, a gentle manner and appropriate humour rather than irony will increase the likelihood that the client will accept what is being pointed out to him in the challenge.

Some ways of challenging

1 Confusing a thought with a fact:
   Example: I'm really ill, I need drugs.
   Challenge: You only think you are ill.
2 All or nothing thinking:
   Example: I'll probably have to go back on them again.
   Challenge: It's all or nothing is it?
3 Exaggerations/minimalizing:
   Example: I'll never be like other people.
   Challenge: What, never?

4 Expecting the worst/predicting the future:
   Example: I just can't do it, everything will go wrong.
   Challenge: You expect to fail.
5 Thinking every situation is the same:
   Example: No matter how hard I try, I can't get it right.
   Challenge: You're thinking this is exactly the same situation.
6 Catastrophizing:
   Example: I'll fall apart.
   Challenge: And then what would happen?
7 Over-generalization/global thinking:
   Example: It would be selfish not to help out.
   Challenge: Are all the people who are not helping, selfish?
8 Projecting onto others/mind reading:
   Example: They must think I'm a real wimp.
   Challenge: How do you know what they think?
9 Self-labelling:
   Example: I doubt whether I have it in me.
   Challenge: You think you are lacking something.
10 'Can't' meaning 'unwilling':
   Example: I can't do anything until I've finished all my work.
   Challenge: Actually you are choosing to finish all the work.

Working with the client in this way changes his thinking to make it more realistic, accepting that people make mistakes, the world is not a fair place and we can neither read other people's minds nor control them. Making the change to more realistic thinking, the client can expect to feel different as a result. It is crucial that the client does not naively replace these distortions with 'positive thoughts' which are actually distortions in the opposite direction. These cannot be maintained and will often be discarded by the client as 'well-intentioned brainwashing'.

Case example

Barbara had been taking antidepressants for six months. She was married with two children in their teens, and worked partly in the home and partly outside in employment which gave her little satisfaction but greater financial security. Her husband had taken many years to set up his own business and he was very concerned about his wife's illness. Barbara was angry with her parents for whom she had never been good enough and who had preferred her brother, although she had been more successful academically at school.

Her mother died a year ago and Barbara had visited her and cared for her conscientiously. Recently it has looked as if her father will soon need more care and Barbara is quite certain she does not want to give up her job and offer him a home with them. She is worried about what other people will think and feels very guilty about being so uncaring. She thinks she is a rotten sort of person.

One of the first distortions for the counsellor to challenge is her husband's belief that Barbara is ill. She had accepted that depression was caused by a biochemical imbalance in the brain and that she was taking drugs to correct this. While it is true that there is a biochemical process involved, this is due to the fact that all our thoughts, feelings and behaviour, good and bad, are biochemically mediated. We are biochemical beings.

Using the psychological model the counsellor sees the cause of this imbalance as more likely to arise out of past experience, life-events and the client's relationships than to have come 'out of the blue' or to have been inherited through the genes. The coincidence of more than one member of a family or several generations becoming depressed does not mean that inheritance is a factor in the 'cause', since the family is a powerful vehicle for learning, and the coincidence of two members of the same family being depressed does not mean a single cause.

Barbara could readily see that the lack of recognition from her parents and the unfairness, lack of satisfaction at work and financial insecurity, the priority of her husband's needs, the death of her mother for whom she had ambivalent feelings and the expectation of the loss of her father, were more than sufficient to provide a cause for her depression or tell her 'what it was about'. She also felt that her depression was justified by the explanation and she now made sense.

Her other distortions were about not wanting to take care of her father and seeing that as 'selfish' and 'uncaring'. Her brother was not seen in the same light and she began to see that there were pressures from her upbringing about what was expected of grown-up daughters. She also saw that she was still trying desperately to please her parents and be good enough. The counsellor also pointed out that while some people might judge her harshly, others might not, and asked her whether it really mattered since it was not other people's job to judge her.

Believing that people at work thought her a real wimp because she didn't stand up for herself was another opportunity for her to mind-read and treat a thought as a fact. She was very angry with herself for constantly worrying about work when she was at home and having to keep checking up that she had not forgotten things. The counsellor challenged her belief that 'I'm so irrational' by explaining that behaviour that comes from feelings rather than thoughts must be irrational rather than rational but that all human beings do it. It is part of being human to have emotions and feelings and not evidence of 'going wrong'.

People feeling anxious and depressed can have become accustomed to having a very poor view of themselves and believe everyone else does too. Low self-esteem and low self-confidence are partly brought about by the loss of a sense of competence and effectiveness and it is vital that counselling works to restore these. Clients can often produce long lists for the counsellor of their real and imagined failings, all the things they cannot do, past mistakes, particularly in comparison with others who are idealized.

One way of working on this is to use the idea of 'strokes' – any act of recognition. Explain to the client that our first experience of 'strokes' is receiving them physically when we are babies and are actually held, stroked and cuddled. As we grow older we receive strokes through smiles, pats on the back, praise or rewards of other kinds. Explain that strokes can be negative as well as positive and in our past we have learned to expect a mixture of the two, hopefully more positive ones than negative ones, although this is not always the case.

Invite the client to talk about the strokes that she received and the balance of positive and negative ones. Does she now expect one kind rather than the other and does she keep out the kind of positive strokes she no longer expects or feels she deserves? Does she feel more comfortable accepting negative strokes because that is what she deserves so positive strokes which might help her have a more realistic view of herself are discounted?

Barbara responded to this hesitantly at first since she found it difficult to trust that the counsellor really did see good qualities in her. It helped to see and understand how hurt and disappointed she had been by her parents' reaction to her and their failure to give her praise for her efforts and achievement. She realized that she sometimes expected her children to be satisfied with the achievement itself and not need anything more from her or their father.

She could see that she was very intelligent well educated and was perfectly competent at her job. She was central to the organization of her family and could see that other people did not always recognize how many demands were made on her, and expected her to know she was loved and valued. A piece of mind-reading she had not engaged in! The counsellor acknowledged her good judgement in setting limits on taking care of others, and suggested that skill could be used to take better care of her own needs too.

It took time and repetition for these new ways of seeing herself to be accepted and not discounted. At first it felt a bit silly and embarrassing when the counsellor said something positive; not at all the sort of thing that British women are supposed to think about themselves, she said. Gradually she came to see that she had written herself off and was tacitly inviting others to do the same. When the counsellor reminded her that she had called herself 'a rotten person' she was appalled to realize what she had been doing to herself when she was so depressed. She never made such hurtful remarks to other people: why herself?

Making sense of feelings

Although some drugs prevent clients working on feelings at depth, it does not mean that feelings cannot be dealt with at all while the client is withdrawing. In fact some clients express their feelings very strongly by talking about them continually, crying, being frightened or irritable. As clients reduce their drugs, feelings can come back in sudden and very powerful ways, which the client has to cope with perhaps for the first time without recourse to drugs.

What the client needs at this stage is to have a way of making sense of himself and his feelings. Where do his feelings come from if, as he is about to learn, people make their own feelings? It is a shift in his view of reality for the client to recognize that he is entitled to have his feelings, and that they are valid for him at the moment he has them. A significant change may be for him to recognize that feelings are not just responses to the present and that factors such as past experience and what is learned through relationships affect them too.

One counselling model which is very accessible and effective with clients taking drugs is Transactional Analysis, partly because it is educational in style and also because the counsellor starts by sharing the model with the client so they have a common language and framework. The client is not struggling to sort out for himself the meaning of the counsellor's model and language at a stage when it is not possible to do that. The clarity which an explanation gives means that counsellor and client are able to examine the client's sense of himself without using their own relationship too soon. The therapeutic relationship will come into its own when it is not distorted by drugs.

The structure of the personality is described by three ego-states, or ways of being, which include distinctive body-language, vocabulary and behaviour. Clients can understand that the brain acts like a video-recorder which is switched on at birth and collects all their experiences throughout life, via their senses. From their earliest days, other people around babies, especially parents, are acting towards and responding to them giving them a sense of who they are, what the world is like and how to survive in it. These beliefs are all stored in the Parent ego-state.

The part of the personality which is concerned with observing and evaluating experience as it happens is the Adult ego-state. Gathering information, checking it, assessing it, making judgements and decisions are all part of the thinking process and are how the person stays in touch with reality. The Adult ego-state acts as the executive part of the person keeping all aspects of the personality integrated and together. The Child ego-state contains all the natural impulses, early experiences, and a person's feelings about himself and other people.

It is unfortunate that these titles for the three ego-states can be misunderstood as being related to a person's age, and it is important to stress that everyone has all three aspects throughout their lives. Most clients can tell when they are feeling child-like, act in a mature way or exercise care or control, and it is important to connect up the theory with the client's experience of himself. Much of it can be drawn from the client who should feel as if Trans-actional Analysis puts into words 'what I already knew'. It is not the end of the story because throughout our lives we are still adding to our stored experience in these ego-states and so we have a theory for change.

In order for the client to access all his ego-states appropriately, he needs to know what they contain, and that there are both positive and negative aspects of them. This provides the client with an opportunity to understand himself in a new way, which is dynamic rather than static, and a sense that he has some choice about how he thinks, feels and behaves. He can work towards increasing the positive aspects and allow the more negative aspects to decrease, giving him both containment and control.

Example of exploring the Parent

In the early work with Barbara described above, she talked about one of her earliest memories being of a time when her mother was in hospital and her father did not come home from work when she expected him to. She described her feelings of terror at the thought that she had lost them both; knowing that she could not live without them she felt totally out of control. This led her to see how she still believed that she could not live without her parents, and explained why her mother's death and father's frailty threatened to overwhelm her.

When she was invited to identify the 'messages' that her parents had given her, perhaps in quite subtle ways, she saw that she had learnt to 'put others first', and that 'men's work is more important than women's'. Because she was quiet and studious her mother called her a 'proper little book-worm' and she began to identify other ways in which she was subtly given 'put-downs' like being teased about her appearance, and began for the first time to feel angry with her parents about what felt to her unfair treatment compared with her brother.

Anger was a feeling that was never acknowledged and Barbara learned that being compliant won her parental approval while being rebellious was evidence of her 'badness'. Father encouraged her to work hard at school, but since there seemed to be no role for a woman with intellect, she had obeyed their 'rules' and promoted her husband's business at the cost of her own career prospects.

She began to see why she was so keen to keep her job because of the recognition it gave her, and was able to acknowledge that was valid and not evidence of being uncaring. Deciding that she did not have to live out the script her parents had written for her, allowed Barbara to think of herself as having a right to discover who she was for herself and stop calling herself 'rotten'.

Example of exploring the Free Child

The counsellor invited Barbara to join in a fantasy journey back through the years to the time when she was very small, perhaps just before she went to school. She was invited to roll back time and remember how the world of her home, playground and family looked to her then and to recall her three favourite things from that time in her life. Barbara relaxed back in her chair and began to smile slightly as pleasant memories came back. She asked what to do with unpleasant thoughts and the counsellor suggested she put those on one side for a while and concentrated on finding good things.

She recalled that one of the things that came to her immediately was reading, and particularly when she was allowed to do it without having to feel guilty that she should have been helping instead. She could recall what her favourite books looked like and the illustrations on the front cover and inside. She could remember playing with dolls and having long conversations with them 'explaining' things to them like going on the bus. The third proved more difficult until she remembered going on a holiday and making mud pies on the beach.

The counsellor explained that this part of her was the natural, spontaneous Free Child ego-state that connected her up with the ways she used to have fun as a child. Barbara replied that she had felt very relaxed when she got into the fantasy. When the counsellor suggested that she probably enjoyed much the same kinds of things now but in more grown-up versions, Barbara could identify having the same feelings when she got into a really good book, not the sort of book she 'ought' to read but one which kept her enthralled.

Playing with dolls seemed a bit like having children, and the counsellor asked her what was good about talking to the dolls and explaining things. Barbara said she thought that what she was really doing was giving her dolls what she wanted – a parent who explained things before you had to do them so that they were less scary. She felt good as a child because she knew she was being the perfect parent that she herself longed for. She had been charged with looking after her younger brother but that seemed harder than the dolls who never made any real demands.

The mud pies were a bit of a puzzle at first until Barbara realized that she liked baking. It was a treat to have all the time in the world to make cakes and pastries, not just the essentials. She also realized that since she had been very depressed she had done very little of that, feeling it was too much trouble. In fact she had stopped doing those very things which seemed to come from her spontaneous self and make her feel satisfied. She actually enjoyed being with her children and doing things together especially when she was explaining or exploring things. She could do more of the things which gave her good feelings to counteract those that were giving her bad feelings.

Getting more out of life

Using an exercise like this to access good feelings in the Child ego-state allows the counsellor to encourage the client to make life-style changes without somehow implying that the client has been getting it all wrong. Giving the client a list of changes that he 'ought' to make might be using the counsellor's Critical Parent to 'tell off' the client's Adapted Child. Transactional Analysis is at its most useful when it allows the counsellor and client to increase a desired ego-state activity rather than decrease an unwanted one.

Boundaries

If you want something new to happen, then first you have to make space for it. One of the reasons why a person may have stopped doing things which give him more satisfaction in life may be that his life is too full already; full perhaps of obligations, duties and responsibilities, or full of other people's lives that are being lived vicariously. Some people begin to take drugs in response to feeling overwhelmed by demands and may have continued to be 'demand driven' rather than 'need led'. The first step then is to make space by setting boundaries around work, the demands of others, other people's feelings and learning to say 'No'.

Leisure

Many clients may have learned early in life that leisure time is wasteful because it is not being useful or that it is something which has to be deserved. Often there is an 'until' script in place which will not allow the person to have any pleasure 'until you have finished your work'. As completion can be an ever-disappearing boundary, the person never gets there. If the client cannot yet sense when enough work has been done and stop, the internal boundary, then guidelines such as 'time everyday for self' and 'three leisure activities a week' can be useful in establishing new boundaries which include leisure as a responsible activity.

Health

Drug-taking is in itself an attempt to restore health, and sometimes indicates a neglect of physical as well as psychological health. The two can never be separate of course, so it is important to consider the part that diet, sleep and exercise can play in restoring a sense of psychological health. These of course, are also related to the set of symptoms of anxiety and depression, and people will benefit from regular meals, good sleep habits and regular exercise apart from the pleasure that these can add to a person's life. It is not the counsellor's role to advocate a healthy life-style *per se*, but to recognize that the client can feel better about himself this way. One way of keeping this clear is to ask 'What were the drugs a substitute for?'

Relationships

Another aspect of the client's present life experience which may be improved while he is still taking drugs is the extent and depth of his personal relationships. Being 'cut off' or socially withdrawn, either as a protective device or an effect of the drugs, is a further loss and steps can be taken to remedy this. It is true that some close relationships may be unsatisfactory, and that will be addressed later, but a first step may be to encourage the client to find and develop new friendships. People need to experience some intimacy and to have a sense that they are liked and approved of by people other than the counsellor.

Passivity

Drugs often have the effect of 'damping' things down and that is why they are used. However good feelings and experiences are lost with the bad, so that clients become fairly inactive. As a means of avoidance the drugs encourage passivity and therefore the treatment should include some ways of encouraging a greater engagement with life. Some of the client's leisure pursuits may be very passive, such as watching sport, television, listening to conversation in a bar, and so on. His life may lack stimulus and have become very boring with little in it to give challenge, achievement and satisfaction.

Taking risks

Withdrawing from drugs is a very risky business for a client because it often means that he is giving up his way of predicting the future and controlling the world. There are no guarantees about this and so the client is faced with taking a risk. Being active in his life and abandoning avoidance as a way of coping will raise the possibility of getting things wrong, being the target of other people's anger or having painful experiences – inevitable in the real world. While he is still taking drugs he needs to make some of the changes which will enable him to live without drugs in the future. These might include confronting other people's behaviour, ending a dead relationship or recognizing when you are on to a loser and giving up.

Wanting

Receiving repeated messages in childhood that wanting is not 'nice', and 'I want – doesn't get', may have led to a suppression of wanting. In fact a client may find it quite difficult to say what he wants out of counselling itself because he is so unused to the concept. His drugs may have symbolized all he was allowed to have and his wanting has been reduced to what was available or socially acceptable. Depression is a successful way of reducing wanting so getting the client to have wanting feelings back and acknowledge them is important. Then the client needs 'permission' to ask for what he wants in direct rather than indirect ways.

Feelings

Just as wanting may be an unfamiliar feeling, so clients may struggle to identify others and name them when they are having them. As drugs are reduced, feelings are re-experienced sometimes fleetingly and the counsellor has an opportunity to help the client notice and identify them. Clients on drugs often cannot respond to the question 'How does that make you feel?' The counsellor needs to get the client to talk about his life in the present in detail, and notice when a feeling is being experienced. Then the counsellor can draw attention to it and help the client name the feeling and locate the feeling in his body. The feeling may be quickly hidden and disposed of by turning it into something else; for example anger may be turned rapidly into hurt and the counsellor needs to spot this.

Accepting others' feelings

People taking drugs may have accepted responsibility throughout their lives for the feelings of others. This is a subtle form of 'Rescuing' because it denies other people the right to make and have their own feelings. Preventing other people from feeling angry, afraid or sad may be what underlies much of the drug use. So the client may avoid other people's anger by being compliant, may prevent other people's fear by being over-protective, may protect other people from sadness by pretending life can be painless. Stopping other people from feeling happy can be a subtle form of punishment which does not have to be acknowledged openly.

Valuing themselves

Somewhere in this process of helping the client get more out of life must come the rationale for it. He is worth it. However that may not be his view of himself and many clients cannot imagine why their counsellor is bothering with them. They make comparisons with other people and put themselves somewhere near the bottom of the pile of humanity. Equality does not mean that every person is the same and hopefully counsellors treat all their clients differently. Equality means that each human being is of equal value with equal human rights and clients need to see that they too have value as people. They have to start treating and judging themselves on the same basis as other people.

Sabotage

Whenever people are making changes in their lives, and in particular when they are reducing their drugs and developing alternatives, they are liable to sabotage themselves. Sabotage means that they undermine their good intentions in subtle ways, often out of awareness. All treatment programmes for addiction recognize this and build in 'relapse prevention' in anticipation that the craving or drug-seeking behaviour will 'counter-attack' the abstinence programme.

Mostly, dependence on prescribed drugs does not produce this craving but people can be just as vulnerable at a psychological level to relapse. Counsellors will recognize that it occurs in the counselling relationship too when clients decide to terminate counselling just as they are experiencing the benefit or sometimes just before. Unrealistic expectations can mean that clients have to reject the counselling which might have given them part of what was hoped for. Setting unreasonably low objectives can be a more subtle way of not getting what you want.

Teaching the client in advance ways in which he or others might inadvertently sabotage himself and how to recognize these ways, means the client and counsellor are more likely to spot sabotage before it does too much damage. This pre-warning 'innoculates' the client to make him less susceptible to sabotage and better able to resist it. Early recognition helps re-start the withdrawal programme or other strategies.

Examples of ways clients sabotage themselves:

1 Starting drug withdrawal before having other ways to cope.
2 Not making any preparations.
3 Not telling other people so they sabotage inadvertently.
4 Telling other people so they can talk you out of it.
5 Making large dose reductions.
6 Reducing again before getting over the previous reduction.
7 Making too many changes at once.
8 Reducing drugs that you need to take.
9 Not asking for help.
10 Accepting unhelpful advice.
11 Making one mistake and giving up altogether.
12 Planning to do it in the distant future.
13 Finding a 'good reason' not to do it.
14 Needing something beyond your control to be different.
15 Only 'trying' to make changes.
16 Doing things to please other people.
17 Not acknowledging your responsibility for taking drugs in the first place.
18 Believing you are special/different from other people.
19 Deciding to protect other people's feelings.
20 Needing a cast-iron guarantee of success.

Sabotage by others

It is not only the client who sabotages himself; other people can join in by suggesting or reinforcing some of the beliefs outlined above. If the drugs were maintaining a particular system of relationships in a family, then some or all members of that system might find themselves disadvantaged by the drug withdrawal and want to find ways to reinstate it. Such sabotage might emphasize the client's illness, weakness, unacceptable behaviour or feelings, and idealize the past health, strength, pleasantness and absence of bad feelings. Examples include:

'You must be ill; you wouldn't have drugs otherwise.'
'You used to be such a happy person.'
'I don't know why you don't just take them.'
'You need something to help you cope.'
'I can't put up with you if you are going to be grumpy.'
'You were a nicer person when you were taking your tablets.'
'Take a tablet; it will stop you going crazy.'
'Those tablets are not doing anything; throw them away.'

The need to keep psychological problems secret from employers and public organizations means that the drug use and the reason for it have become something about which people are ashamed. Even when it is quite clear that the medical diagnosis was superficial and the treatment inappropriate, clients are easily sabotaged by the fear of being found out. Some employers still see demands for '110 per cent commitment' as evidence that they only employ 'high-flyers' rather than evidence that they abuse their employees. In this case sabotage is likely to result from attempts to meet unrealistic levels of perfection or avoid failure. Examples include:

Employers
'These are your targets; I know you can cope.'
'Look, if you are not up to this . . . .'
'We don't have any passengers.'
'You've got the wrong kind of personality.'

Employees
'If my employer found out it would ruin my promotion chances.'
'I have to get a good night's sleep.'
'I need something to stop my hand shaking.'
'If they knew I was seeing a counsellor . . . .'

Among the unexpected saboteurs are the general practitioner and the counsellor. Doctors can undermine by taking responsibility away from the client by prescribing alternatives or temporary help which suggests that the client cannot manage alone. Undermining the efforts and skill of the counsellor by referring to it as 'a bit of a chat' or 'well it can't do any harm' can be disarming when accompanied by a warm smile. The counsellor can feel alarmed if the client does not seem to be progressing as fast as the counsellor hoped, and apply pressure. Challenging the medical model, especially at first, leaves the counsellor on unsafe ground and she may suddenly mistrust the client. Examples include:

Doctors
'I'll just give you something to tide you over.'
'I don't think it is advisable to dig up the past.'
'Counselling? All mumbo-jumbo to me!'
'There is no reason you should have to feel so upset.'

Counsellors
'Haven't you come off your drugs yet?'
'Well just give it a try.'
'I don't know about drugs, you'd better ask your doctor.'
'Other people don't have this difficulty.'

Rescuers and Persecutors

One way of describing the process of sabotage is in terms of the Drama Triangle model in Transactional Analysis (Stewart and Joines, 1987; Johnstone, 1989). There are three game-playing positions: Victim, Rescuer and Persecutor. The two players adopt two of the positions, usually starting with the client in Victim inviting the doctor or counsellor to rescue them: 'Do me something' or 'Wooden leg'. This is an invitation to sabotage the client by doing for him what the client could do himself. The pay-off comes when one player moves to the vacant position, usually Persecutor, and the other one collects bad feelings.

If the doctor or counsellor makes the switch, the client feels persecuted and punished: 'Well, I didn't really expect you to succeed.' 'If you'd taken my advice, none of this would have happened.' 'I suppose I shall have to give you some more tablets.' If the client switches to Persecutor the doctor and counsellor can feel punished: 'You told me I should be better off.' 'I'm not taking your advice again.' 'I told you I was really ill.' The way to stay out of the game is for both parties to make decisions from Adult. The client is the person who at some level knows what is best for him and must take responsibility for making decisions.

Relapse

All the processes of change, life-style as well as drug use, will come up against obstacles, temporary set-backs and retreats. Therefore it is important to build it into the process so that when it is encountered the client is not thrown off his stride and gives up. It should not be seen as a failure if it is anticipated and can be reframed as a useful learning experience just as the former attempts to reduce drugs were. All learning involves making mistakes. The following questions need to be worked through:

1 What went wrong and why?
2 How does the client feel about himself?
3 Was the former plan realistic?
4 What is realistic now?
5 How should it be done differently next time?
6 What changes are necessary first?
7 What is possible for client and counsellor?
8 Does the contract need to be changed?

Progress so far

Reaching this point in the counselling means there is an opportunity to evaluate progress with the client. The client should have learned how to manage the drug withdrawal for himself, made several reductions and coped satisfactorily with the withdrawal symptoms without recourse to further prescribing. Secondly counselling should have made significant inroads into the distorted thinking and self-awareness of the client, and helped him to meet his needs with alternatives to drugs. Having implemented this, the client should be comfortable and confident about continuing this programme and expect to succeed.

There is also an opportunity to review the original objectives and for the client to decide whether this is all he wants. Sometimes a client withdraws from counselling at this stage until he is completely off drugs and can review things again. Even if his drug use was quite small and he has come off by this time, it may be all the client is seeking. If he wants more, will he be continuing with this counsellor or seeking a different experience elsewhere? Sometimes an experience of group therapy is what the client wants and coming off drugs was a condition of entry.

If the client decides to continue counselling, he may be ready to move on to the next stage. Clients who are ready are likely either to be off antipsychotic drugs or on low doses of benzodiazepines or antidepressants. It may be possible for a client taking antipsychotic drugs to benefit from some of the work in the next chapter, but the depth of work will still be limited, so the counsellor should set herself realistic objectives as well as sharing this knowledge with the client. For example it is important to work with the issue of loss, but mourning cannot be considered to be completed while antipsychotic drugs are still being used. The next chapter describes how change is maintained and the focus moves away from drug withdrawal towards counselling for the underlying issues.

5

Maintaining the Change

Psychotropic drugs are a crutch, so the real goal of any withdrawal programme is not abstinence itself but being able to maintain it. The focus of this third stage is therefore towards helping the client maintain himself drug-free for the future. This may mean dealing with the long-term effects of the drugs by re-learning lost social and life skills and coping strategies. Clients who have taken benzo-diazepines or antidepressants will need to talk with the counsellor about the first prescription to explore what was being avoided then.

The client needs to make sense of the past way of seeing his problem medically and to re-think it in terms of what he should or could have done about the problem then. Even if the prescribing has been useful, the client has to start looking for real solutions. This may mean thinking the unthinkable, saying the unsayable, or doing the unacceptable, at least as the client has previously judged it.

By this stage the counsellor may expect that the client has begun to make connections between his past experience and recent events or current relationships. In terms of the counselling model described in Chapter 2, the work can move from the focus on thinking, feelings and behaviour towards examining the dynamic relationship between past and present. It is a move towards helping the client to see the meaning he puts on events or relationships and that these can be understood in terms of his own past experiences particularly in early life.

The counselling style is able to change from a more prescriptive to a more exploratory one with the client starting to identify patterns in his life, repetitions of previous relationships or re-enactments of the past. The 'messages' encoded in infancy can emerge into awareness or unconscious conflicts can be recognized. The client is able to dream again, making that a rich source of material for those who work that way. Metaphors and images can be used creatively with the client who can 'go inside' to see if things fit.

The relationship between the client and the counsellor begins to have greater significance in counselling because the counsellor can use what happens in the session to help the client identify his expectations of others. It is particularly important to recognize that clients who have depended on a substance to help them feel better need to explore dependence patterns on others and the counselling relationship provides an ideal setting for that.

Excessive conformity

It is vital to the infant's survival to please his parents, and at any price. Keeping the parents 'good' means that when the child experiences bad feelings with the parents, the child assumes that 'it must be me' who is getting things wrong because it is impossible for me to survive with 'bad' parents. This leads to the child adapting his behaviour to fit in with what seems to be expected or to please the parent, and internal conflicts are dealt with by suppressing desires and conforming to parental expectations instead. There are several models of human development which describe this process.

This process is the means of identity formation and social learning. Conforming to external standards and norms in order to gain approval has its place in childhood, but counsellors may notice that many clients who have been prescribed drugs for anxiety, depression or stress have behaviour patterns which indicate that they had to be excessively conforming to get the necessary approval, or that in fact they never managed to feel that they were approved of at all. An overwhelming desire to please others is pathological.

Clients in counselling often express their sense of alienation from society by saying that they are not normal, not like other people, or by pointing out how much they deviate from some understood norm of behaviour or feeling. People who have taken drugs for a long time may give as one of their reasons for wanting to withdraw the desire to be 'normal again'. The idea of normality was developed during the person's early life and the feeling that he is 'out of step' was sometimes a significant part of the reason for seeking medical help. The drugs may have been used to make the individual conform to his own ideas of normality.

Other people are often idealized as 'happy', 'getting on with their lives', 'coping better than me', 'don't seem to have any problems' – that is, 'normal'. The client may then have judged himself a total failure in these respects and used drugs to make himself more acceptable. Social pressure may reinforce this with definitions of what is acceptable or unacceptable for different people in a variety of situations. Deviation from the imagined norm is then pathologized into being 'sick'.

Transactional Analysis provides the counsellor with a useful and very accessible model for exploring conformity. The Adapted or Conforming Child ego-state contains all the messages the person received in their early life about ways to cope under pressure. There are five 'Driver' behaviours which everybody uses from time to time when they are under pressure but most people have one or two preferred ones. It is helpful for the client to see how useful to us these Driver behaviours can be sometimes when they fulfil a positive function, but that they can have a negative effect too.

Drivers	*Negative message*
Be Strong	Don't show feelings
Try Hard	Don't stop
Hurry Up	Don't think
Be Perfect	Don't be satisfied
Please People	Don't grow up

However the counsellor works, it is important not to attempt to over-rule these Driver behaviours without recognizing that they have performed a vital role in allowing the client to survive so far. The first step is to explore with the client the fears of psychological annihilation through going crazy, falling apart or being rejected or abandoned that may underlie the Driver behaviour. The injunctions which accompany each Driver probably protect the client from the threatening injunction 'Don't exist' by allowing them to survive as long as they 'Don't show feelings' or 'Don't grow up', for example. Case examples of how to work with each personality adaptation are described in Ware (1983).

Drivers and prescribing

BE STRONG

People with this Driver have learned in childhood that feelings should not be expressed and that being angry, sad or afraid is unacceptable to other people. They may even believe that other people rarely have such feelings themselves, and that these are evidence that they are weak or bad in some way. It is possible that the prescribing was used to suppress emotions and clients may have been prescribed following bereavements to control sadness and crying, to contain the anger in depression or to control the fear in anxiety.

TRY HARD

No matter how hard they tried to please their parents, approval for people with this Driver was always withheld, often in order to encourage them to keep on trying. Parents may have been afraid that the child would become lazy if left to work at his own pace and constant chivvying and poking was used to keep the pressure up. Whatever the child did was not good enough so they had to keep trying. It is subjecting themselves to relentless pressure that led these clients to take drugs 'in order to relax' because they were addicted to trying and putting all their investment into effort rather than achievement.

HURRY UP

Time is the pressure that people with a 'Hurry Up' Driver subject themselves to, and they probably experienced impatience from their over-stretched parents in some way. They often set themselves far too much to achieve in the time available and are sometimes the victims in abusive employment with increasing demands for productivity to unrealistic time-scales. They rarely have time to stop and think and are particularly prone to seek 'quick solutions' with the hope that they are also simple ones. The prescribing fits easily into this pattern since it avoids the necessity to spend time looking for real solutions.

BE PERFECT

Perfectionism and the demand that nothing is good enough unless it is perfect was often the message that these people received in childhood. A strict upbringing, over-rigidity on the part of the parent may produce an inhibited over-conscientious person who suffers from tension. The prescribing may keep them conforming sometimes in obsessive or compulsive forms and rituals. They can often find that letting go their high standards for themselves and having fun is difficult. Being ill might be one way that the client had of accommodating his less-perfect performances, and the prescribing was a way of confirming this.

PLEASE PEOPLE

It does not take much perceptiveness to spot that drugs are sometimes given to one member of a family when somebody else has a problem. They are used often to avoid conflict and to keep an impossible situation stable. Unsatisfactory relationships especially when they are symbiotic, may be kept going by the removal of the feelings of merger and the unsatisfactory dependence redefined as 'closeness'. Drugs may be used to encourage passivity and an illusion of detachment or control feelings of hatred and destructiveness.

The over-critical Parent

Clients whose language is full of 'shoulds', 'musts', 'have to' and 'got to' alert the counsellor to the need to examine the beliefs they have about themselves and how to survive in the world. These beliefs laid down in their childhood reflect the parenting they received, often from rigid, moralistic restraining parent figures. Clients may still be obeying rules they have never been given permission to modify. Many clients were brought up in an era when parents were afraid to 'spoil' a child by meeting his demands and attention was strictly rationed.

The 'infantile rage' may have been directed against the self and the person become self-critical, self-denying or self-destructive. These clients set themselves unrealistically high standards which they do not set others, and then criticize themselves when they fail. Quite often the counsellor can be aware that these clients are expecting to do all the therapeutic work themselves and keeping the counsellor out. They may also be very angry with themselves for their inability to see in advance what is revealed by counselling.

Giving clients like this a positive view of themselves is often difficult because they reject anything which does not fit their negative self-image. The counsellor has to work gently at pointing out when their criticism of themselves is unreasonable and derived from their past messages. A startling change can occur when the counsellor agrees that a particular behaviour was not alright and gently criticizes it. The client can discover that he is not diminished by such realistic criticism and can survive intact as a person.

The art of criticizing depends on a few fundamental principles to make it acceptable and useful. These are:

1 The criticism should comment on behaviour not the person.
2 It should be owned as an opinion not disguised as a fact.
3 It should be about something which can be changed.
4 It should be specific not global.
5 The reasons why the person holds that opinion should be given.
6 The desired behaviour should be specified.
7 It should be done in a respectful manner, not intended to humiliate.

In order to cope with being criticized, clients must first distinguish between realistic criticism of their real errors or failings and unrealistic criticism which is inaccurate or designed to humiliate. The person being criticized must decide 'Is it true?' That step immediately puts the experience within the client's control: they decide. Having decided whether the criticism is true or not, the client accepts what is true and disagrees with what is not true. Clients are often amazed to realize that they have been accepting all criticism, true and untrue.

Realistic criticism

1   Accept it:
>   'You're quite right, that is a messy piece of work.'
>   'Yes, I could have told you I didn't want to do it earlier.'
2   Ask for information, accept it:
>   'What is it that I do which irritates you?'
>   'What have I got wrong?'

Unrealistic criticism

1   Reject it:
>   'No, I'm not feeling grumpy.'
>   'No, I'm not trying to wind you up.'
2   Ask for information, reject it:
>   'When did I promise you that?'
>   'What is the evidence that I'm a lazy person?'
3   Use fogging. Confuse with vagueness:
>   'You may have a point. Maybe . . . Oh, do you think so . . .?'

The surfacing of anger

Anger may be directed against others, doctors, government agencies, pharmaceutical companies, and this is particularly the case when the client has suffered severe distress in dealing with his dependence. Many clients do experience difficulty withdrawing from benzodiazepines because of the time it takes, the withdrawal syndrome and the disruption to their lives. Many suffer a loss of esteem at having to recognize their dependence on a substance perhaps because they would prefer to deny their need for dependence on people.

Occasionally the client becomes very angry with the counsellor, the focus being around the drug dependence problems, but this may be a disguise for the anger about his unmet dependency needs in childhood. Commenting on this dynamic between past and present dependency may help the client to recognize it and deal with it with the counsellor. Unfortunately if the client is not yet ready to recognize where his feelings of vulnerability are derived from, this may provoke even greater feelings of rage. It can be a no-win situation: commenting on dependency needs can provoke further anger, failure to do so leaves the client searching for answers that are not there.

Case example
Brian had been taking benzodiazepines for seven years for panic attacks, and while he was coming off his drugs he had been very angry with everyone and blamed the drugs. When he had been off his drugs for four months, the counsellor suggested that all the people and things that Brian had been angry about were the target of his anger not the cause. He began to see that his panic attacks might be the result of his suppressed anger and that he had expressed it through his criticism of drugs, doctors, counsellors and so on.

Brian said he had been thinking about the last 10 years and could see his paranoia in thinking that his colleagues at work thought him a wimp and were planning to get rid of him. He thought that the counsellor saw him as silly and a nuisance, and criticized him just as mother had. When he was young, she had not liked weak, sensitive, emotional people, pushed him to be successful, gave him no recognition and had a dreadful temper herself. He began to see how he had felt punished and humiliated.

Much of the work in the next few months focused on the conflict between his sensitive, gentle side which was very idealistic and wanted to put his ideals into practice in his work, and his desire to kill off the weak and vulnerable part of himself. In the counselling relationship he expressed a longing for dependence, followed by an angry rejection of the counsellor for being incompetent, and manipulating him.

He demanded to be told that it was all to do with the drugs and not him, and when the counsellor would not confirm that, he was angry and critical. As the symptoms improved, he was able to express anger in a more controlled way and he got positive feedback from colleagues. He said he was learning from experience that his needing to be in control all the time was the problem and not the drugs.

He made connections between his mother's envy about her un-lived life and the belittling of his father. He recognized that a lot of what went on in counselling was really about defending himself from the counsellor doing to him what his mother did to his father, and what his mother did to him. As he made these connections he was able to feel his vulnerability and cry. Then he was angry with the counsellor again for failing to be the expert he wanted, for being too weak and vulnerable to take care of him. He was angry because he had to protect the counsellor from being crushed or defend against her retaliation and that meant that there was no one powerful enough to take care of him.

Finally he began to explore how his battles with his mother were being re-played in the counselling. He realized how much he had wanted to please her and win her love while at the same time wanting to prove her wrong. He was able to talk with considerable insight about his ambivalent dependence on the counsellor matching his ambivalent dependence on his mother, and the conflict with the belief that 'men are the strong ones'. He realized that his anger was a way of getting close to his mother as well as a way of feeling separate from her. The final session contained the important insight that he was no longer afraid panic attacks would kill him and for him that was a landmark.

Comments on the case example
While Brian was still on benzodiazepines, he was very angry with his weak, dependent self and that showed itself in panic attacks which he found life-threatening. He was impatient, irritable and dismissive of himself and focused all his attention on the symptoms. He used the withdrawal protocol rigidly and he was determined to 'tough it out'. All the bad feelings were projected out on to other people: his employers for their plots to sack him and the doctor and counsellor as they alternated in the 'bad parent' role.

When Brian had been off benzodiazepines for about four months, there was a gradual recalling of his mother's temper and punishing and humiliating behaviour towards him. He started to integrate the two sides of himself, his dependent and self-sufficient selves who had been 'fighting it out'. Although he was still angry and critical with the counsellor, there was evidence that the anger was being expressed outside the counselling in a more controlled way. He recognized that he had been symbolically fighting his mother for control and was able to contact the hurt under his rage.

The ending phase marked the realization that anger for him was a form of closeness and emotional contact that made him feel real and energized. When the anger was out, the symptoms could no longer kill him. A holiday break brought about the discovery that the counsellor like his mother, would not always be there to rely on and he made his decision to separate and become self-reliant. Finally he used anger to separate from the counsellor and reinforce his sense of independence.

Psychological needs

Reading psychological self-help books is a popular and useful way that clients can continue the process of change in their lives. One such book (Pitman, 1991: 9) makes the point that 'we are all, in fact, rather like a business organisation. We receive lots of inputs (attention, recognition, information about others' expectations of us). We have to decide how to develop the business (personality, attitudes, feelings), and how to behave towards our colleagues (decisions, beliefs, behaviour). . . .' People taking drugs have often been so busy 'pleasing their customers' in the business of living their lives, that they forgot to adequately resource 'the workforce', that is themselves.

Pitman goes on to say 'In life, as in business, we may be successful (liking ourselves, fully developing our talents and skills) or we may break even (living safely, but dully) or even go bankrupt (making a mess of our lives, going crazy, killing ourselves)' (1991: 10). Clients in counselling might see themselves as having taken drugs because they made a mess of things or were living too safely and now want to be more successful. If however the client is going to stay in business in the long term, he will need to learn to like himself as a 'good enough' not perfect person.

A significant number of clients have taken drugs in order to suppress their own needs, and in order to over-supply the needs of others. When the drugs are withdrawn they can often see this pattern yet be reluctant to change it because, for example, they have been socially conditioned into that role, and feel guilty giving themselves a higher priority. This may partly explain the greater number of women than men who take psychotropic drugs. Yet these clients have the nurturing skills, but they mostly direct them towards other people. If the change from drug use is to be maintained, the client has to be more aware of his own needs.

Staying with the analogy of running a business, a good manager is one who can recognize and meet the needs of the workforce. In return the manager gets maximum cooperation and loyalty from the workforce. Perhaps the client can recognize the need for a good internal manager to make sure needs get met and the business of living is successful. Some of the needs of the workforce are set out in *Social Skills at Work* (Fontana, 1990) and include:

1 Appreciation – the recognition and valuation by others of our efforts and abilities.
2 Significance – closely related to appreciation, this is the sense that we matter as people.
3 Power – related to significance, people need the power to affect decision-making in key areas of their lives.
4 Usefulness – related to significance, individuals need skills and abilities that are of use to the community.
5 Acceptance – acceptance by others of who and what we are, rather than constant criticism.

6 Understanding – sympathy and understanding from others concerning our problems.
7 Direction – clear guidance when we require it.
8 Space – a necessary minimum of personal freedom and privacy.
9 Leisure – free time and the relaxation that goes with it.
10 Companionship – friends and acquaintances with whom we can talk and share interests.
11 Stimulation – an element of variety and distraction in our lives.
12 Progress – a sense of advance and achievement, or of working towards some identifiable goal.
13 Coherence and pattern – some consistency, structure and meaning in life.
14 Happiness – positive emotions and a sense of being in harmony with ourselves and the world.

   The counsellor's task is to help the client recognize and state his needs, clarifying thinking, exploring feelings and changing attitudes and beliefs. This can be done at three levels.

Early life

1 Which of these needs were met or unmet in childhood?
2 How and by whom?
3 Were the person's needs met fully and willingly?
4 What messages was the client given about himself when needs were not met?
5 How was the client taught to get his needs met elsewhere in healthy or unhealthy ways?
6 What external factors such as illness, war, divorce, poverty etc. meant that some needs could not be met?
7 What lessons did the client get in self-care?

When drugs were first prescribed

1 What needs were not being met then?
2 Did the drugs meet needs or suppress them?
3 What early lessons was the client still applying to his life?
4 Were these still useful or appropriate?
5 What part did relationships or social expectations play?
6 What changes would have satisfied these needs?

When drugs have been withdrawn

1 What needs can the client identify as emerging?
2 Does the client recognize these as normal for adults?
3 Does the client accept responsibility for meeting his needs?

4 Can he leave other people to be responsible for themselves?
5 How is the client planning to meet his needs in healthy ways?
6 What self-care will he introduce to maintain a drug-free future?

Acknowledging feelings

Prescribed drugs have the effect of dulling or blunting the emotions, and were probably used to make feelings more manageable when the client felt in danger of being overwhelmed psychologically. When the drugs are withdrawn, feelings gradually re-emerge allowing them to be experienced, explored and expressed appropriately. However drugs were a defence and without them, the client at first feels vulnerable and undefended until he has developed sufficient experience that having feelings is survivable.

At first some clients cannot name a feeling and the concept in Transactional Analysis of four main sets of feelings, 'glad, mad, sad and scared' is a useful starting point. It helps the client to understand that fear is a feeling about future loss, sadness is an acceptance of past loss and anger is a feeling in the present that defends against loss. The good feelings are experienced in the present and being the antithesis of loss are about feeling securely attached. Realistically it is not possible to have only good feelings and to have them all the time.

It is not surprising that a client who has not been in touch with feelings for the last 20 years or so should be somewhat bewildered by the therapeutic question 'How do you feel about that?' Asking a client how he feels is sometimes premature and shifts him into a cognitive mode where he starts to *think* about how he feels, and is confused. A more helpful approach is to invite him to describe past events in as much detail as possible. Leading the client to realize the implications of what did or did not happen helps him discover the *meaning*. Discovering the meaning, he may begin to experience a feeling, which the counsellor can reflect.

As well as linking past and present in the session, the counsellor may also use what occurs in the relationship between herself and the client. Feelings experienced in the 'here and now' can be identified and explored for their meaning. Learning to notice the feelings as he has them is important for the client who may then transfer this ability into the rest of his life outside counselling.

Time for self and leisure

Drugs used to suppress needs so that the client could take care of the needs of others, may also suppress the resentment that must accompany such a loss. As the client becomes aware of wanting to meet his own needs, he may have to overcome the social conditioning that such behaviour is selfish. The word 'selfish' has a negative connotation and the client may struggle to re-frame 'selfish' behaviour as self-care, and morally responsible.

Fundamental to this change is a more egalitarian view that helps the client to value himself as he has previously valued other people. Valuing himself the client becomes entitled to experience good feelings in life to balance out the inevitable bad ones. Privacy, time for oneself, control over the demands of others, as well as satisfying leisure pursuits, means the client making space for changes to occur. Other people especially partners, are often more encouraging of these changes than former drug-using clients anticipate. If they are not, the problem may belong to the partner.

Stimulus and challenge

Another effect of taking psychotropic drugs is that of increased passivity and a loss of confidence. Loss of confidence is frequently the loss of a sense of competence not self-esteem, although the two are closely connected. Avoidance, handing over problems to be solved by another and the sedative effects of drugs all encourage passivity because the symptoms no longer provoke discomfort and the client does not have to do anything about it. Once off the drugs the client needs help to become active again to channel his energy into demanding and satisfying work.

Work gives people a challenge, structure, relatedness through a shared task, a chance to develop a part of themselves previously unused. The mind no longer dulled by drugs can think and learn again, enjoy a sense of making progress, achieve new goals, develop a sense of powerfulness and control over life. Many women make up for past lost educational opportunities, getting out of an old rut and leaving the domestic environment that no longer gives them meaning and satisfaction. It is an opportunity for men too to re-think where they are going in life and set new goals.

Sexuality and intimacy

Since reduced libido and sexual dysfunction are common side-effects of drugs, when sexual feelings return some people experience a rebound effect, that is their sexual interest is increased. This new awareness of their body, touch and sexual desire prompts some clients to search for a sexual partner in a way that may seem quite promiscuous. Psychotropic drugs can be both inhibiting and disinhibiting, but when suppressed sexual desire emerges it may feel overwhelming.

This is one area of the client's life where a partner cannot be ignored since the change in the client involves adjustment by the partner. This may be dealt with by the partner being invited to join in the counselling. Such a decision needs to be carefully thought through, and worked with not only by the counsellor and client but also by the client and his partner. New goals and boundaries have to be established and it is probably better to do this towards the end of the counselling process since it changes the nature of the client–counsellor relationship.

Case example

When Tim came for counselling, he had been taking benzo-diazepines for 17 years. He had reduced on his own for two years but had found coping with the increase of symptoms difficult to tolerate and his drinking had escalated to between 40 and 50 units of alcohol a week. While reducing, he had noticed an increase in libido and because he found it unacceptable to 'keep pestering my wife', he found relief in masturbation. He agreed to keep taking the drugs while working on the alcohol problem, but after six sessions he halved his dose of diazepam, and three sessions later stopped altogether. He experienced many and severe withdrawal symptoms, violent dreams, incontinence and numbness in the groin.

With the drinking under control, as he went deeper into his past to understand his 'illnesses', his eating problem surfaced and he experienced intermittent strong sexual urges. A short break in the counselling gave him the opportunity to re-evaluate the problem and Tim put sexuality and finding a meaning in life as his objectives. He had been talking to his wife, and realized that he expressed his feelings through his symptoms, because there had not been space for him to have his feelings in his family of origin.

Tim thought he and his wife were at opposite ends of the sex-drive continuum, and began to explore the reason for that. When he told her what he was discussing, she 'bridled' at first and they thought about the possibility of counselling together elsewhere. Meanwhile they had started to explore the sexual difficulty, and Tim would bring to his counselling what his wife said about herself.

Since they seemed to have got started, they asked if Laura could come with Tim to join the counselling. Laura realized that she had never been allowed to grow up to be a sexual person, and with Tim's support, she started to read books that helped her find her sexual self. Tim found Laura taking the lead in sex difficult at first and feared he would not be able to fulfil her expectations.

They talked a lot every day, discovered a new meaning to their relationship and after three months started to look at their parenting difficulties because the sexual problems 'felt finished'. Two more months were spent working together on their children's problems and then Laura and Tim decided that Laura would leave and Tim continued his counselling for a further two months.

Tim felt that Laura's joining the sessions had speeded up his counselling and that they had been able to talk about parenting issues together. Laura thought that it had been liberating to find her sexuality, and she had learned a lot from watching Tim and the counsellor. From the counsellor's perspective, Laura's joining the sessions had worked and they had found a much deeper level of relationship.

Issues of dependence

Dependence in the present

Clients who have been physically or psychologically dependent on a drug, often have other examples of dependence in their lives. Sometimes it shows up in other members of the family. When the drugs are stopped, unless the underlying issue is recognized and dealt with, the client is still vulnerable to re-dependence. Some people have withdrawn from one prescribed drug only to substitute another or to self-prescribe. The current drug dependence may represent only one link in a long chain of using substances in this way.

Recalling that for clients taking medication, counselling is always their second attempt to get help, the dependence on someone else to solve the problem re-emerges as an issue and must be addressed. Being dependent on doctors to know what is best or over-compliance that sometimes goes with extensive psychiatric histories, suggests that the counsellor should look deeper into the client's past to see where these patterns originate.

Some clients may still be tied to symbiotic relationships with their parents, unwilling to separate without the 'permission' of the parent. The inner conflict that was suppressed by drugs may have been about the ambivalence the client experienced over attempts to leave. Alternatively if separation was partially successful, the client may have maintained emotional dependence while setting up a dependent relationship with a partner. Partners who seem over-involved or over-protective may suggest that significant work on dependence still needs to be done.

The fourth area where dependence may be a problem is in the relationship with the counsellor. This is more obvious with the client who starts off being very demanding, constantly contacting by telephone, dropping in to a clinic or asking for extra sessions or time with the counsellor. Less obvious is the absence of healthy dependence in the client who does it all himself, doesn't want to trouble the counsellor with questions and makes little or no reference to holidays or other absences making any impact on him. The client who never challenges the boundaries even when he may clearly need more support, may have an inability to attach which the counsellor could easily overlook.

Attachment in early life

These two forms of insecure attachment − clingy or self-sufficient − are described in Attachment theories of neurosis as 'Ambivalent' and 'Avoidant' attachment (Holmes, 1993). Counsellors will already have heard the life story of their client and can probably identify the symbiotic relationship, the physical or emotional absence of either parent, events such as death, separation, illness or time in hospital, which prevented or disturbed the client's secure attachment.

Attachment theory makes the connection between parenting which produces secure attachment and the process of psychotherapy which offers the client a chance to re-work the attachment with the counsellor. There are three components in the counselling: attunement, the fostering of autobiographical competence and affective processing. These correspond closely to Rogers' empathy, honesty and non-possessive warmth as the three core conditions for therapeutic change.

If the client's dependence on a substance is an indication of insecure attachment in early life, then that is the underlying issue which this period of the counselling needs to address. The drug use did not address this issue but merely replicated it, by encouraging dependence or denial and avoidance. Thus drug use may have prevented any of this re-parenting taking place while the drugs were being taken. Withdrawal of the drugs is likely to expose the client once more to his anxieties about insecure attachment.

Psychotropic drugs affect the 'attunement' by making it difficult for the counsellor to make contact with a person who is not fully 'there'. Counsellors often experience the cut-off relating style and clients describe feeling out of touch or free-floating and distanced from everybody. Problems of memory recall and information-processing prevent the client making sense of his life experience, and loss of affect means affective processing cannot take place. Therefore the counsellor is not starting from where the client was when he was first prescribed but from further back, because of having to re-activate lost psychological processes.

Panic attacks and agoraphobia

It is likely that many clients will already have done some work with the counsellor on these symptoms not only because they are often part of the reason for the first prescription but also because they are common side-effects of psychotropic drugs. Benzodiazepine use, for example, increases the incidence of the symptoms and they are common withdrawal effects.

Most work will have been done at a cognitive and behavioural level by exploring the client's unrealistic beliefs relating them to present reality. In addition the client has probably been confronting his fears by practising doing the difficult journey or being alone, rather than avoiding it. These are useful and necessary steps but incomplete without work at a deeper affective level. Behavioural changes are not easily maintained unless deeper levels of counselling are attempted after withdrawal.

Attachment theory helps the client to see that panic attacks and agoraphobia are really about the insecure attachments of his early life. Much of his present life may show traces of that insecurity if not parallels to it. For this he will need a new experience of secure attachment which is what the counselling must provide. As the past insecurity is dealt with the client may be able to 'grow up' from his current symbiotic relationships, discover his competence and learn to accept his feelings even if they are negative ones.

Dependence on the counsellor

Some medical services offering help with psychological problems and drug use see dependence on the counsellor as 'neurotic' and actively discourage it. The client may have switched his dependence on his drugs into dependence on his counsellor and find the counsellor's attempts to disengage frightening or even persecutory. A client learning to overcome his reluctance to form closer attachments may pick up the counsellor's signals that this attachment is unwelcome or unhealthy and withdraw again. In attachment theory, 'dependence on the therapist is not seen as inherently neurotic, but as an appropriate response to emotional distress' (Holmes, 1993: 153).

Holmes describes the therapist's task of providing a secure base as including compassion and caring as well as clear boundaries. Clients with ambivalent attachment styles need absolute reliability, firm limits and a push towards exploration. Clients with avoidant styles need a flexible and friendly therapeutic relationship with very respectful interpretations. The therapist needs to seek and accept attachment as a goal in itself and this is particularly important with clients who have a more disturbed attachment style.

Promoting separation

It follows from an understanding that issues of dependence are really issues of attachment, that the way to promote separation is first to promote attachment. It is when the need to form a secure attachment has been met by the counsellor that the client is ready to separate and go on to form successful attachments in the rest of his life. This means that the counsellor must respectfully accept the strong positive feelings of the client who is seeking to attach while reflecting back the responsibility and competence in the decision to seek counselling. In the same way, strong negative feelings can be accepted as having some basis in the present as well as the past, without the counsellor provoking separation to relieve her own discomfort.

There are two things which need to be kept in balance. First the counsellor has to encourage healthy attachment without enmeshment. This will mean that the client has not been Rescued and is able to leave the counsellor when the time comes. Secondly the counsellor has to encourage competence and independence without provoking premature separation. This will mean that the client has not been Persecuted for his natural desire for attachment or allowed to regress to a false self-sufficiency. It is the counsellor's task to manage the boundaries and maintain an appropriate distance between the two of them without Rescuing or Persecuting.

For the ambivalent client:

1   Reliably returning telephone calls, particularly during a crisis or when the client needs to check on drug reductions or withdrawal symptoms.
2   If the calls are too frequent, suggesting that the client can get support from family and friends too, and reminding him of his competence. Agreeing the interval before the client makes contact again.
3   If the client asks for extra sessions or longer sessions, not allowing that to happen by default, but listening to the client's reasons for the request and responding to the reason on its own merits.
4   Acknowledging from the beginning that there will be an ending, either by fixing the number of sessions or if the contract is open-ended, by agreeing that the counsellor will not end unilaterally.
5   Not spacing sessions out nor being increasingly unavailable to promote separation by stealth.
6   Modelling competence for the client while supporting the client's self-esteem when he expresses vulnerability.

For the avoidant client:

1 Inviting the client to telephone if necessary for information or advice, rather than making mistakes or letting things get much worse.
2 If the client is struggling to do it all alone, reminding him of his responsibility and good judgement in seeking counselling in the first place.
3 Offering extra sessions if the client needs more 'holding' and checking at the end of a session in which the client has been in touch with difficult feelings, that he has a few moments to compose himself before leaving.
4 Reassuring the client if a fixed number of sessions is available that further counselling will be discussed at the end, or if it is open-ended that the client will know when he is ready to end and the counsellor does not expect the client to end before then.
5 Challenging premature attempts to end, while not leaving the client feeling that the counsellor is dependent on him to fulfil all her interpretations or hopes.
6 Modelling attachment for the client, while inviting him to use the counsellor as a consultant with whom he can share his inner life.

Adjustment to loss

The exploration of people's need for attachment points also to the importance of dealing with loss. It is the anticipation of future loss which is anxiety and the defence against past loss which is depression. That is what most clients have been using drugs to cope with. Many of them will have expressed their emotional distress in terms of loss of control or loss of relatedness, depending on how they see it.

Giving up drugs constitutes a further loss before there have been many recognizable gains, so the client may have depended on the counsellor to point out each small step forward. However nothing can protect a person from experiencing the inherent loss in giving up what he used to cope, what made life manageable for a while. The drugs have been part of the false security which the client used to bolster his self-esteem, and the gap between relying on drugs or self means the client taking an enormous psychological risk.

Quite often the most difficult dose reduction that the client makes is the last one. There is considerable anecdotal evidence that suggests that clients withdrawing from benzodiazepines find stopping the last tablet particularly difficult. This is not a pharmacological problem. Reassurance that the last dose is only a homeopathic amount, cutting the tablet into ever smaller and smaller pieces, dissolving tablets and watering the solution down, replacing with placebos, substituting with something else, are all likely to collude with the avoidance of the real moment of truth – starting to trust oneself.

As drugs have been reduced the client has been re-exposed to his anxiety and depression and the counsellor can work with the underlying feelings of loss as they emerge. It helps the client to re-affirm for himself that he is not and never has been 'ill', in the sense that in some way anxiety and depression are unexplainable. Working through his life-history, making sense of it and attaching the appropriate feelings of fear, anger, sadness and joy, may help to make his reaction understandable and acceptable. The client can gradually learn to deal with his personal material without fear of psychological overwhelm.

Loneliness
Being emotionally cut off for months or years means that the client experiences a loss of a sense of himself as well as a loss of others. He may not recognize himself at first or find it difficult to see himself in relation to others. Feelings of vulnerability can be heightened by the sense of aloneness which is experienced as 'in here' or 'out there'. Passivity may have led to a reluctance to approach other people, a fear of engaging with them as if he is scared of living.

The loneliness may be due to actual isolation which was previously unnoticed. There may be no partner, no peers, no adult friends in his life. If life on drugs has been centred solely on employment or child-rearing, it may come as a surprise when the client realizes that he not only has no friends but has forgotten how to make friends and maintain friendships. It is much easier to leave things as they are and stay in the sick role. In that way isolation does not have to be confronted or partners can be expected to fulfil all social needs. Otherwise the client may have to take the risk of testing out whether he can matter to other people.

Bereavements
All psychotropic drugs, including antidepressants, interfere to some extent with the mourning process, even if used in low doses, or for some other purpose, and even if the client believes that he has mourned fully. Single doses of a benzodiazepine at the time of death will affect what the client is able to fully experience and much will be beyond recall in future because it was never fully stored in the memory. That is not recoverable, and is the reason that no psychotropic drugs should be prescribed at the time of death or at

the time of funerals because those who are bereaved need full awareness. Drug-induced sleep may seem superficially desirable but talking about the loss restores calmness without unwanted effects. Naturally occurring shock is what protects people and they need no further pharmacological intervention.

When drugs are removed all past losses resurface and mourning can continue. Any losses which occurred during the time of the drug use may need to be mourned for the first time. Some grief work can be accomplished while the client is taking antidepressants but must be incomplete until after the drug is stopped. Clients taking antipsychotics and benzodiazepines may appear to have grieved since they may have cried a lot and still be expressing sorrow. However their grief will be protracted and unresolved. More commonly grief is inhibited and the client is left in denial.

Deaths are not the only losses to be mourned but much of the natural life experience too. People will have moved houses and jobs, worked hard and missed out on fun, lost their grown-up children from the home or retired from work altogether. Sometimes the original reason for the drugs was postnatal depression and the losses associated with becoming a parent must still be acknowledged. People who have had surgery and lost organs and limbs need to grieve for those too. Sometimes the grieving is displaced onto a well-loved pet, and the focus of the grief can seem trivial, but what matters is the meaning or significance that is attached to the loss.

Loss of life experience

At the end of drug use the client is confronted with the loss of his life while he was taking drugs. What is past cannot ever be re-experienced. It may be too late to make some changes and the client may feel very angry with himself for inadvertently allowing his life to be stolen 'while his back was turned'. A life lived without finding a sense of health and well-being may leave the client angry with other people or too angry to admit it to himself. Making changes reminds him that he could have made these changes before.

If life has passed him by, he may not recall significant family events such as births and deaths. Some women whose children are leaving home find it a poignant moment when they realize they have missed out on the experiences of raising children. Not being in charge of one's life, giving part of it away because it was too painful, might have seemed a good idea at the time but it is very hard to redecide that before it is too late; it is the price of living defensively.

Couples may have drifted apart without noticing, and if not actually separating, they may have lost emotional closeness and intimacy. It may be too late to change that and the partner may have built a life of her own. It is the looking back and questioning what life has been used for that can prove to be very painful. 'I didn't do anything with my life, never travelled, never studied, never made anything of myself, never achieved anything.' It is the echo of finality as the door shuts irrevocably on an unlived life, which may haunt the person until she grieves for it. Life has no dress rehearsal; there is no second chance.

Fear of death
It has been said that all anxiety is ultimately about our own death. We may deny or ignore that, but life contains repeated reminders that in spite of the pretence of immortality, there are no exceptions. In practice the only way to cope with this knowledge is para-doxically to live as if we are immortal. While the client is experiencing a panic attack and thinking, 'What if I should die?', he is defended from minding about it. Sometimes at moments of great misery death may have seemed a release from suffering.

Without drugs, death begins to make an impact again and a person can find television or newspaper reports of death and suffering threatening to overwhelm him again. It is as if he cannot separate feelings about himself and other people and needs to establish some distance from other people's suffering. This may be a response to his own insecurity and the counsellor needs to help the client accept his fears. Religious certainties which were once a comfort may now prove inadequate and the client is forced to re-evaluate his belief system to encompass doubt.

Conclusion

At this stage in the counselling the client has dealt with his drug use fully, not only withdrawing from the drugs but also overcoming the long-term effects of them. In addition the underlying cause of the symptoms has been identified and worked through. Finally if a secure attachment has been made by the client to the counsellor, the counselling can address the fundamental psychological needs.

Throughout, the client has been practising new skills, growing in awareness and developing confidence by being responded to by others. These are transferable to the client's life outside the coun-selling session. The counsellor may be aware of other issues not yet dealt with, which form part of the client's story. These may not have been considered in the assessment perhaps because neither was aware of them. The return to reality means they need to be addressed by the counselling.

6

The Return to Reality

Now that the client no longer experiences the blocking effects of his drugs, the underlying problem may emerge. With antidepressants the problem has already been accessible. In a way the client is in danger of finding himself back at the beginning, just where he left off with the first prescription. However that is not really true, since much of the work that he has been doing in the counselling so far will be pertinent to the underlying problem too. It is not surprising however if some clients when they have finished the drug issues, feel dismayed at finding there is yet more to do.

Most of what emerges is unwelcome initially: finding one's true self, having to take responsibility for the past, the present and the future, having to deal with all the things the client hoped he had got rid of. Denial is no longer supported by drugs, defences are removed, the client is exposed to the harshness of reality. It is not surprising that symptoms may re-emerge as anxiety, depression or insomnia, and tempting for the prescriber to offer another drug 'which will deal with the real unrecognized depression'. This would mean a replication of missing the real problem in the first consultation.

Since drugs 'bury' the problem and it becomes 'unburied' when drugs are withdrawn, the client is often prepared for material related to the time of the first consultation to return. For example if the client has taken benzodiazepines for 15 years, he may expect to have to work through all the events of those 15 years and what occurred in the year or two before. What often surprises him and the counsellor is that the 'unburying' does not stop there but goes right back to infancy. It is as if everything which could not be processed by the immature child and got 'forgotten' becomes available to recall and this can happen quite suddenly.

Success at this stage of the counselling depends on how deeply the counsellor has been able to engage and interact with the client throughout the relationship. If the client senses the attachment is insecure he may either separate prematurely, perhaps assuring the counsellor that all his counselling needs have been met, or demonstrate excessive neediness by a return of the symptoms. The counsellor must not be deceived by this into thinking that some underlying psychiatric disorder has been identified, and that this work will be beyond the counsellor's competence.

The client needs to know that the counsellor is prepared to stay with him while he faces the possibility that what emerges will be unexpected, possibly frightening, overwhelming again, saddening or enraging. What is least expected is what sometimes happens: nothing. Not that there is nothing to deal with; rather that try as they may, neither client nor counsellor seems able quite to get in touch with what has been suppressed. They need to give it time and gently work to facilitate what the counsellor knows from experience needs to be done. The client may need reassurance that the counsellor is not impatient about getting on with the work.

The post-withdrawal syndrome

This syndrome applies mostly to benzodiazepines but some aspects may be useful and relevant to the withdrawal of other drugs. When the client finally comes off drugs, and experiences the last withdrawal reaction, he may still experience what seem like withdrawal symptoms occasionally and intermittently. Reassurance from doctors that this is not a true withdrawal reaction may be true but leaves the client without any way of making sense of his symptoms. First, he needs to know that this experience is shared by others and is quite common. Secondly, he may be helped by an understanding of what may be happening biochemically.

Psychotropic drugs work by inhibiting or enhancing the effects of various neuro-transmitters. Withdrawal of the drug means that the blocking effect of an inhibitor or the increased effect of an enhancer is no longer there. It takes time for the body to restore itself to normal levels of these chemicals and for the resulting psychological adjustment to take place. This is a two-way process, so that the work the client does in psychological terms will have an effect on his biochemistry. The post-withdrawal period may be quite protracted and individuals vary considerably.

It is important therefore that the client is prepared for this rebound effect and expects that he might at first feel worse. In addition he is experiencing events and reactions that he may not have fully experienced for quite a long time. The skills he once had will have got 'rusty' through lack of use and have to be re-learned experientially. Until the chemical adjustments have occurred, the client may feel very vulnerable in a world that suddenly seems louder, brighter and faster than he recalls, and an inner world that feels strangely unfamiliar too.

An extreme form of this post-withdrawal syndrome occurs when a client has been withdrawn from drugs abruptly or too rapidly, or when he has been withdrawn without counselling. In view of the fact that psychological adjustment to coming off drugs is complex, many people who have withdrawn in self-help groups will come into this category. These groups provide encouragement and support but are insufficient in providing objectivity and challenge. They are effective in giving people part of what they need and aiding the drug withdrawal but self-help groups cannot be expected to provide therapy.

When withdrawal is done too rapidly there is insufficient time for a withdrawal reaction which is manageable to occur and subside before the next reduction is made. A second reduction before the first has been experienced and accommodated leads to a build up of delayed withdrawal effects which can overwhelm the client. Rapid withdrawal leads to an increase in the number and severity of symptoms and these include hallucinations and psychotic episodes. These more complex problems will be dealt with in Chapter 7.

Advice to doctors in the medical guidelines about rates of withdrawal errs on the side of over-optimism. Recent changes have moved to correct this, but some doctors have been left over-pessimistic because they believed they were following the guidelines correctly. Guidelines do allow that 'counselling may be helpful' but omit to say that it is probably essential if a full recovery is to be made. Because the symptoms occur much later and are not ascribed to poor judgement about the rate of withdrawal, they are often ascribed to some inherent defect in the client's personality or a psychiatric disorder such as panic. Perhaps it has more to do with the doctor's anxiety and excessive haste than the patient.

The counsellor faced with a client who has withdrawn too quickly may be tempted to pass the problem back to the doctor to solve. A better approach may be to work together to consider all aspects of the difficulty and to include the client in the exchange of information. One choice is for the client to stick things out and continue to work in the counselling sessions on building the necessary skills and new ways of coping with increased support. The problem with this is that it may not be possible for the client to tolerate the symptoms and he gets into a cycle of panic which is difficult to break. Going back on the drugs then becomes a bigger failure.

A second choice is to go back on a lower dose of the same drug, wait for symptoms to stabilize again and proceed with a more gradual rate of reduction. One problem is that some drugs once withdrawn seem to lose their effectiveness when taken again, so it may not work and have to be undone again. It is important if drugs are re-started, not to reinforce the belief that drugs are a solution to the client's problem and this is where cooperation between the doctor and counsellor is crucial. It is also difficult for the client who has blamed all his problems onto drugs to go back on them again. Alternative prescribing does not work and merely adds to the problem.

The client who has 'successfully' withdrawn without any counselling can be particularly resistant to the idea that he needed to do anything further. It is a very difficult time to start counselling anyone and frequently leads to unsatisfactory outcomes. Many counsellors may have no choice but to attempt to work with clients that have already been made worse by colleagues. It may help the client to be absolutely honest about this but it may not do much for relationships with colleagues, so measures to prevent it recurring probably need to be put in place as tactfully as possible.

There are issues the counsellor has to address by identifying what is unspoken about what has gone wrong, accessing the unexpressed feelings and discussing them with the client in the session. These may include:

1 The client's beliefs about being ill, drugs, needing external solutions and his right to be cured may still be intact.
2 The client may not have 'owned' responsibility for his part in it.
3 He has experienced a failure and may feel disappointed and angry.
4 He may have already tried many alternative therapies which have not worked leaving him exhausted and de-motivated.
5 The behaviour of demanding attention and instant results while being very mistrustful may mask the actual desperation.
6 He is vulnerable to being Rescued but it must be by a 'higher authority'; psychiatry or going privately are particularly attractive.
7 He may be at risk of acting out his desperation through using excessive alcohol, over-dosing, leaving home, resigning or threatening suicide.

Pathological grief

Grief which is inhibited, protracted or chronically unresolved is pathological, and all clients who have suffered losses before or while taking psychotropic drugs will have been affected in the mourning process to some extent. Antipsychotic drugs and benzo-diazepines inhibit grief work either from starting or continuing. Mourning may continue for some people while they are taking antidepressants but the grieving cannot be considered to be complete until the drugs have been withdrawn and all the suppressed emotions have been expressed.

The counsellor may become aware quite early on in the relationship that losses have not been fully resolved when the client reports that he 'soon got over it', did not really seem to need to grieve or had no feelings. Where the grief seems to have been transferred onto another loss such as a pet, or where the present reaction seems out of proportion to the extent of the loss, it may be that the current loss has triggered grief from previous unresolved losses. A third indicator of pathological grief is continual crying which does not seem to bring relief. The crying is happening but it is 'crying for' (i.e. searching) rather than 'letting go' (i.e. acceptance).

In a research study into the reasons why people were prescribed benzodiazepines (Hammersley and Hamlin, 1990), 19 per cent of those studied had been given their first prescription following a bereavement, and as they were gradually withdrawn from their drugs re-connected with their grief again. In addition the coun-sellors discovered that all subsequent losses had to be mourned too, sometimes going back over a period of 25 years.

Problems were encountered for those clients who had been prescribed immediately following the death because they had not processed the events and many details were lost for ever. Where the prescribing occurred later because grief was misdiagnosed or given an inappropriate remedy, details of the death and funeral could usually be recalled. However there were significant gaps in what was accessible to recall after many years of drug use.

Whether or not the grieving process starts on its own when the client is reducing drugs, the counsellor needs to make some assessment of which grief 'tasks' have not been done. There are four 'tasks of mourning' (Worden, 1982); and these are first to accept the reality of the loss, and this must be done on all psychological levels. Secondly the bereaved must experience the pain of grief, and all the emotions including guilt, anger and sadness must be released.

Worden describes the third task as adjusting to an environment in which the deceased is missing, and for this the client has to develop new skills. Most of what was covered in Chapter 5 covers this adaptation to changed circumstances. The fourth task is to withdraw emotional energy and re-invest it in another relationship. This is the stage which is reached after the client has finally engaged in the 'letting go' weeping described above, which allows him to move away from the previous attachment without dishonour and frees him to re-attach again.

So the client who has withdrawn from his drugs may have completed to some extent task three but by using drugs, missed out part or all of tasks one and two. The counsellor therefore needs to address these tasks rather than being led by the client into moving onto task four and omitting them completely. To do so would compound the pathological adjustments the client is attempting. The client may at first resist this expecting that there will be no further benefit until the part drugs play in preventing grieving is pointed out. An unwillingness to encounter the pain again is evidence that the grief remains unresolved.

Some ways to facilitate grieving:

1 Retelling the story in as much detail as possible.
2 Focusing on forgotten events and searching for contextual triggers, e.g. Where were you living then? Who else was there?
3 Suggesting the client talks to other people about the loss or talking to other witnesses to fill in the gaps.
4 Reading letters of condolence, newspaper reports of the funeral, death certificates, wills etc.
5 Looking at photographs and handling memorabilia of the deceased.
6 Disposing of or redistributing the clothing and personal effects of the deceased.
7 Marking significant events, relationships or the work of the deceased, e.g. performing a last duty as a parting gift to the deceased.
8 Writing a letter to the deceased if there was no farewell.
9 Visiting the cemetery, grave, chapel of rest, erecting headstones, or making gardens etc.
10 Visiting places associated with the deceased, e.g. former homes, scene of death, church of funeral service.

Emotion is released not by asking the client about his feelings but by noticing throughout this work when feelings seem to be near the surface and reflecting them back to the client. This is a way of letting the client know what it is appropriate for him to feel. It may require first a safe and holding relationship (a temporary secure base) so that the client can take the risk of letting go emotionally, without fear of abandonment or loss of self-esteem. After the first experience of the relief which this expression of emotion brings, the client should be able to recognize that it is what he needs to repeat.

Case example

Stephanie was a widow in her early sixties who came for counselling because she could not get over her husband's death following an operation to remove a brain tumour. He had died unexpectedly several days after the operation which she had assumed he would survive and she had not been with him at the bedside and had not said goodbye. Her husband had died about two years before and she had been taking the sleeping tablet (benzodiazepine) triazolam, 250 micrograms since soon after his death.

Much of the counselling focused on her adaptation to her new life, spending time in the same home, in contact with her three grown up children, still socializing with the friends she and her husband had shared. When she accepted that triazolam was preventing her grieving – and it was the chronic superficial weeping which convinced her she needed to access her deeper feelings – she decided to withdraw gradually. This she did in two stages while on visits to family abroad because then she was very busy with grandchildren and slept better.

After she had been off for a while she realized that she had little idea of how her family had experienced the loss of their father or how her friends felt at the loss of a man well known in the community. She started to raise the subject with them and gradually built up a better picture of the final few weeks of his life with her. She had been so busy with the plans for the operation that she had missed out on noticing what was happening for her husband though her children had noticed. They shared with her their father's thoughts and concern about her, and she was deeply moved by this.

Gradually Stephanie started to talk again about the days after the operation when her husband seemed to be doing so well. She was able to acknowledge how she felt about the indignity to her husband of wearing a wig, and how on finding the wig in a drawer again she had been glad to throw it away. She confessed to discovering that he sometimes looked very tired in hospital when he did not know she had arrived and was looking at him, and that now she felt guilty that he had had to protect her.

Eventually the gap appeared since Stephanie did not know how her husband had died and who had been with him and suddenly she needed to know that. The counsellor suggested writing to the consultant – who when he talked to her after her husband's death, had offered to be of further help – to ask him these questions. Stephanie was unsure whether writing to consultants was really allowed, but she realized it might help and she brought a copy of her carefully constructed letter to show the counsellor who reassured her that it was fine.

The weeks passed without Stephanie getting a reply and she had all kinds of fantasies about how outraged the consultant had been or that he had been just too busy to notice and reply to her letter. The counsellor suggested writing again because Stephanie had invested so much hope in the reply that it seemed better to get a rebuff over which she might feel angry than to have no reply at all. A response came immediately from the consultant, saying that he had been abroad for two months and his secretary had not forwarded her letter.

He wrote very personally about his memories of her and her husband and Stephanie was deeply moved to realize that after two years the consultant still remembered him. He talked about his surprise and sorrow at her husband's death and how he had had to grieve too when he had wanted and expected her husband to survive. He mirrored some of her anger that the death had been untimely when in every other way her husband had been so fit and active. She felt that at last someone else had felt as she had and that helped.

Finally he told her that at the time her husband was dying he had had a nurse with him throughout holding his hand and talking to him. He offered Stephanie the opportunity if she wanted it, to write to the nurse to ask her for her memories. He said that he was pleased Stephanie had written to him and hoped she would write again if there was anything further she wanted to know. Stephanie brought the letter to show her counsellor and cried about it. That was the turning point and she was able to complete her grieving and let her husband go.

Post-traumatic stress disorder

When counselling a client who appears to have experienced a traumatic event before the prescribing, the issue is still loss in some form, only that it has been expressed somatically. Therefore the treatment approach is the same as for facilitating pathological grief: recall of the events, narrative competence and affective processing. In particular there are some issues that need to be dealt with specifically: a comparison between what should have and what did occur immediately after the incident and consideration of the consequences of the failure to obtain a correct diagnosis.

What is different for the counsellor is how the problem is presented. After all the client and counsellor are making a retrospective diagnosis together as a result of the drugs being withdrawn and the client is making a connection between his physical and psychological symptoms and a previous traumatic event. It often depends on the new information from the counsellor that physical symptoms of 'stress' do not usually surface until between six months and two years after stressful events or combinations of events. That is often the piece of information that was missing when the doctor discounted trauma as a possible cause of the symptoms. It is worse when trauma is known to be the cause and drugs are wrongly prescribed for example for insomnia.

People can be involved in critical incidents in a variety of ways, as company employees or agents, passengers or customers, public service employees or bystanders. The incident can be major, requiring the involvement of many people and watched over and reported in the media, or minor with little involvement of others. Ideally those involved will be de-briefed in groups and across groups as soon as possible and within 24–48 hours, and not dispersed home. Often there is confusion, relatives arrive and become involved or some people are separated by being dispatched to hospital or continuing their journey.

Some of the themes which may be worked on include:

1   What information was offered immediately or was it withheld and by whom? What did that mean for the client?
2   Was talking to other people who were involved at the time discouraged or facilitated? How did other groups of people such as the crew, police and bystanders experience the same event?
3   How does the client think he coped? Was he helpless or competent? What fantasies does he have about the staff who cried or those who showed no emotion?
4   What responsibility does the client still feel and who has he blamed? Is he still waiting for court hearings or compensation?
5   What feelings did he have about being out of control, abandoned or about to die?
6   How did the client respond to other people's handling of the incident? Was he angered by false reassurances or grateful for everyone's kindness?

In the aftermath of the event the client may still have been in shock, which is a natural insulation against the enormity of the event and will have minimalized the extent to which he had been affected. The denial may have been reinforced by relatives relieved at survival and wanting to encourage a quick recovery. Guilt at surviving or not being as badly injured as others may make it difficult for people to recognize the impact on them. Drinking alcohol, smoking or asking for sleeping tablets all contribute to the denial of trauma. Offers of counselling, telephone helplines and support groups are frequently declined because people do not recognize their need and others discourage it.

Unrecognized trauma

The client who has been taking drugs, and then realizes that he experienced a traumatic event which he has not dealt with, has often been through an extensive range of medical treatments. There has either been no diagnosis or a changing one depending on the specialty of the person referred to, and there may have been a variety of interventions which have been largely unsuccessful. It is therefore useful to consider, when this scenario is described in the first consultation, whether this client has experienced an unrecognized traumatic event. The scenario of course does not definitely diagnose such trauma, but it is one of the possible options.

Example

1 The emergence 6–24 months after a traumatic event of a symptom such as over-alertness, tinnitus, feeling of coldness or heat, unspecific pains or rashes. If the client is already taking drugs the flashbacks, nightmares, hallucinations and phobias may have been suppressed and physical symptoms are more likely.

2 The symptom is treated often with a benzodiazepine hypnotic and/or the patient is referred for investigation.

3 The symptom does not respond to drugs, or is removed and replaced by a different symptom or the symptom gets worse and there are new symptoms.

4 The investigating specialist, i.e. ENT surgeon, neurologist, cardiologist, gastroenterologist, dermatologist, finds no organic cause, prescribes for the symptom and/or refers the patient back to his general practitioner with a suggestion to try another specialty. This is repeated several times.

5 Other 'problems' that the patient did not know he had are identified and treated, e.g. high blood pressure, high cholesterol levels, menopausal symptoms.

6 The patient begins to worry about the unrecognized and unspecific illnesses and mistrusts reassurances since there is no explanation of the symptoms and they are getting worse.

7 The patient starts to feel that he is a nuisance or difficult to treat and suffers from 'fat-notes syndrome'.

8 The anxiety is diagnosed as depression, seen as a cause not a consequence and the patient is referred to a psychiatrist and/or prescribed antidepressants.

9 The increasing polypharmacy may worry the patient who seeks help from a variety of alternative therapists both helpful and harmful.

10 The patient stops taking some of his drugs abruptly and suffers a reaction which confirms the view of the physician that he 'needs' the drugs, and the view of the patient that there is now something wrong with his 'nerves'.

Sometimes in this scenario the client has seen a psychologist with a medical frame of reference who replicates what has been done by doctors and the client is left to conclude that the problem is not psychological either. In spite of there being no diagnosis and no organic illness, prescribing can have occurred at any stage of the process, confusing the issue and complicating the treatment. The specialists have rarely admitted that their diagnosis is not definitive but an educated or sometimes an uneducated guess, and nobody has really listened to the patient.

The difficulty for the counsellor may be that either she is part of the medically orientated system and cannot challenge it, or she is outside it and does not know enough about the processes to challenge it. The first hypothesis that the symptom had a physical cause has to be rejected in order for the counsellor and client to explore the idea that the traumatic event is really the origin of the symptom: and not really the event itself but the fact that the client's traumatic experience has never been psychologically processed.

It may be very difficult when the client first comes to seek counselling – often as a last resort and reluctantly – to acknowledge this, and being free from drugs may help the client to view his past treatment in a new light. Part of the difficulty may be around having to reject so much care and helpfulness when he first sought help or feelings of guilt about not having responded to treatment and pleased people.

Later persecutory experiences of being discounted may have led the patient to become more determined that a physical explanation should be found so that he would not be thought to have been inventing it and wasting everybody's time and money. The client is in danger of feeling gullible at having been taken in as well as silly not to have told anyone before now what was a probable cause of the symptoms. It is important that the counsellor acknowledges the desperation that drove this search for a solution and allows the fears of ME, cancer, brain tumours and other worries to be expressed and accepted.

Obsessions

If the client was having obsessive thoughts before he was prescribed, they can be expected to resurface again when the drugs are stopped. The prescribing merely dealt with controlling the obsessive thinking and compulsive behaviour; it did not allow access to feelings and the meaning of the symptoms. If the client did not have this symptom before drugs were prescribed, it may come as a surprise from an un-buried past. It is not a new psychiatric illness nor does it need to be treated separately from the on-going counselling.

Some counsellors may feel out of their depth dealing with these unexpected thoughts and be tempted to abandon the client as beyond their competence. It is better to seek expert supervision than refer the client on to someone who may in fact be less competent to deal with it and with whom the client has to start again. Cognitive behavioural approaches may be a way of containing the symptoms and are less risky than alternative treatments which offer brief or rapid solutions through removal of symptoms.

Obsessive thinking may be a psychological symptom indicating a traumatic event or period which has been suppressed. Going deeper into childhood to access the unresolved feelings and the meaning behind the obsession, it is important to remember that it represented the best explanation and solution that was available to the child at that time, given his level of maturity. It may take time to access its meaning because of the strange quality of magical thinking around issues of safety.

Some ways for counsellors to explore the meaning of the obsession:

1 *Perfectionism*: a way of being good, or keeping the world good, which defends the child against feelings of badness, sinfulness and evil.
2 *Rigidity*: a sense of deserving punishment and a fear of divine retribution which is held at bay only by enacting the ritual exactly.
3 *Secrecy*: there is an injunction about talking about things, possibly because it will bring harm to others, or there was nobody to tell.

4 *Abuse*: evidence of physical, psychological or sexual abuse, and self-destructive behaviour such as cutting.
5 There is a close connection between substance abuse, sexual abuse and eating disorders (which may be thought of as an obsession). Where there are two in evidence, it is likely that the third is present in close proximity to the client.

Childhood sexual abuse

Both male and female clients during the process of post-drug-use counselling may recover memories of sexual abuse, although characteristically they may not at first correctly identify it as such. When the counsellor begins to suspect that the client is presenting a sexual abuse survivor scenario, it is appropriate to enquire whether the client has any memories of people behaving towards him or her physically or sexually in ways that felt strange or wrong. This does not implant the idea, but makes specific the fact that the counsellor is aware that what the client is describing may fit such a past history.

Draucker (1992) describes a dynamic model of the trauma-producing factors in sexual abuse from Finkelhor and Browne (1985) as follows: traumatic sexualization, betrayal, powerlessness and stigmatization. These factors have their counterparts in the pathology of the sexual abuse survivor, which may be evident only when the drugs are withdrawn, but are what the counselling treatment has to address.

The long-term effects of traumatic sexualization are described as precocious, aggressive or indiscriminate sexual behaviours, or sexual dysfunctions, sexual identity confusion and sexual avoidance. These last three – sexual dysfunction, identity confusion and avoidance – may be masked by the drug use but the withdrawal of the drugs may highlight the past abuse through the emergence of precocious, aggressive or indiscriminate sexual behaviour.

The long-term effects of the betrayal are identified by Draucker as isolation, disturbed interpersonal relationships, further abuse and aggression. Again the drug use may have both masked and replicated the isolation, disturbed interpersonal relationships and abuse through the substance misuse. When the drugs are withdrawn the repressed anger which was identified as aggression may come to the surface again but what is most significant is the difficulty the client may have in being able to stay in a trusting relationship with a 'significant other' or authority figure.

Nightmares and flashbacks (usually suppressed by drugs), low self-efficacy and under-achievement are the long-term effects of powerlessness and may produce compensatory behaviours such as aggression and delinquency. Clients may show this in exaggerated reactions to being touched even in non-sexual ways or in delinquent behaviour such as shop-lifting. The drug use may have masked issues of powerlessness because accepting medical help involves handing over power to the prescriber and the drug itself may produce dependence and passivity. The work described earlier in countering adaptiveness and unassertiveness and increasing expectations of success and competence will increase self-efficacy.

Drug use may have replicated the process of stigmatization for the client, just as previous attempts to disclose the sexual abuse may have done. Not being listened to, not being understood and being dismissed as naughty or 'neurotic' may have contributed to the client's sense of disorientation and worthlessness. Feeling in some way to blame for the abuse, the person may have developed an overwhelming sense of guilt, have feelings of shame associated with wanting, and a dislike of being watched.

Case example

Angela was divorced from her husband who had had an alcohol problem and been violent towards her, and now lived alone in a flat not far from her widowed mother with whom she still had daily contact. She had one grown-up daughter who still maintained contact with her father but lived elsewhere. After her divorce she had come for counselling to come off diazepam on which she had been dependent for many years, primarily because she had developed severe agoraphobia and was extremely anxious.

She had been part of a group and had learned many useful skills during her withdrawal and felt that the agoraphobia would finally go when she had stopped taking diazepam. However she could never quite manage without it, and found that she was afraid to go out of her flat apart from going to her part-time job or her mother's, but when she tried to stop she was overwhelmed with a terror of being left alone especially at night.

She had joined a dating agency and had some bad experiences discovering that the dates she met only wanted to have sex with her. Nevertheless within a few days she would get a call from a 'really nice man' and she would agree to go out on a date with him after checking that he knew that she wanted to be friends only, for a while. At the end of the date he would come back to her flat and she would become terrified of him leaving and beg him to stay with her but in a platonic way. They would finish up having sex together, he would reassure her that he did not think she was 'easy' and she would not hear from him again.

The next day she would feel dirty and worthless and appalled at her promiscuity, and would then see that the signs had been there for her to see but she had been deceived again in not spotting her 'date' was only looking for sex. She would decide that she was not going to make any more dates that way but in a few days the pattern would start again. She longed for a relationship but seemed unconsciously to be replicating patterns of abuse.

As the nightime terrors were explored, Angela came to realize that her fear of being left alone, her inability to judge the motives and intentions of others and the difficulty she had in maintaining the boundaries she had set suggested that she had been sexually abused at some time. Gradually she had day-time flashbacks of sitting on her uncle's lap and of him stroking and fondling her. Not having a father at home she had enjoyed being his special 'girl' and the treats he gave her.

At first she did not recognize it as abuse until she recalled a memory of him holding her too tight and pressing her against him. She now realized with grown-up insight how confused she had felt when he became sexually aroused and would not let her get off his lap although she had not liked him being breathless. Exploring the context of the abuse helped Angela to realize the long-term effects the abuse had had on her.

It also began to make sense of the failed marriage in which she had been unable to set boundaries, her powerlessness in the face of sexual demands, her lack of judgement when her wants were in conflict, and her overwhelming sense of shame. It cast a new light too on the diagnosis of 'anxiety attacks', the reason for the original prescription.

The angry family

When one element in a dynamic system changes, something else will have to change to accommodate it in order to restore the equilibrium. Drug use is one way of maintaining the family dynamic by keeping one person in a particular role or allowing the individual or family to maintain a belief. The individual discomfort with a role or belief may have been removed by drugs and so removed the necessity for other people to change their roles or expectations.

It is the lack of stability in the family system which provoked the first consultation, and the prescribing produced a 'false equilibrium' which is lost when the prescribing is stopped. This change may have a 'domino' effect, producing liberating changes for other members of the family if they are willing to make changes too. If they are unwilling to recognize their part in it, have too much invested in the client remaining the same, have too much to lose if the client changes, then they may resent the disequilibrium being exposed and be angry.

Some families or partners may attempt to sabotage the client once it becomes clear that coming off drugs and counselling are going to have implications for them. One way they may do it is to get the 'sick' member of the family back in the sick role again, and there were examples of that in Chapter 3. All the client's attempts to talk about problems are personalized into the client's pathology again; feelings are evidence of not coping.

Secondly they may tell the client that what he is doing in counselling is not an improvement; they preferred him the way he was. They may threaten to destabilize the family by leaving home, seeking a separation, attempting suicide or in other more subtle ways, such as becoming ill themselves and blaming the client. Finally they may blame the counsellor or the counselling for 'upsetting' things in some way. All of these may be signs that the family is denying or avoiding facing issues which have previously been kept under wraps.

Dead relationships

What may be a painful realization for the client is the discovery that he has been maintaining a number of dead relationships. Grown-up children may have to be thrown out of the home, dependent parents may have to take responsibility for themselves, partners may not be in love with the client any more than the client is still in love with them. Love may have died a long time ago and the drugs have only been propping up the empty shell and postponing the ending.

The decision may then be made to stay off drugs, find a new identity and purpose in life, acknowledge that relationships die and end it. This may mean having regrets, and working through the loss before starting again with a new vision. If the price of ending the relationship is too high, the client may return to drug use again, but the counsellor should confront this so that the client is aware of what he is doing. Sometimes it is the client's honesty and willingness to risk everything that wins him a chance of a better relationship.

Endings

In addition to the ways that counsellors normally end with their clients, clients who have been taking prescribed drugs may need something else. After they have come off drugs and worked through the underlying issues, they often cannot tell how much is there to be dealt with. In order to prevent 'hanging on in case', which would undermine the client's new-found confidence and competence, the client may need reassurance that this is often the case, but that the client can end anyway. They will need to know that they can come back again if other issues surface to get further counselling or a referral elsewhere.

In ending it needs to be acknowledged that the client never 'needed' drugs in the first place, that the drugs may have been helpful in the short term, but the long-term gains they have made have all been due to their own efforts not the drug. Clients can then see that they have really learned something that they will go on using and that they will continue to grow as people after the counselling has ended. In fact there are some things they cannot have from counselling until it has ended.

The third thing the client needs to hear is that the decision to accept staying on drugs or to risk coming off was a mature decision. Asking another adult for help through counselling is an appropriate thing to do and not evidence of weakness. In this way the client can undertake responsibility for his future drug use or abstinence. Since much of the early work will have involved working in a very confronting and directive way, it may be important to acknowledge that the counsellor appreciated the client's decision to allow that.

Conclusion

This chapter has brought the counselling relationship to an end, with the drugs accepted or withdrawn, the long-term effects dealt with and the underlying issues resolved in some way. The client's drug use has been re-evaluated in the light of the counselling work and there is some realistic expectation that the client will not return to inappropriate prescribed drug use for psychological and social problems. By integrating the two issues the drugs were not withdrawn without regard to the part they were playing in maintaining some equilibrium, nor was the counselling undermined and made ineffective by the drugs.

The final chapter deals with some of the complex areas where counselling and prescribed drugs may meet, identifying the part drugs play in helping or harming the counselling. There are some guidelines for counsellors handling these complex situations but it would be rare for anyone to be acting alone, and supervision or consultancy is vital. Many of the situations pose complex ethical dilemmas since different professions working together may have different views of ethical practice. Clarifying her own perspective is crucial for the counsellor.

7

Some Complex Areas

This final chapter will not apply to all clients because it is not about a part of the counselling process. It deals with some areas where drug use and counselling come together, either because the drug use is at the centre of the problem or because it is easily overlooked. It describes what the counsellor needs to know and where to get more information, what to do or not do, and when to refer on. It may mean a reversal by which the counsellor is referring to a doctor and counsellors are sometimes unsure when it is appropriate.

It covers specialist areas of counselling such as eating disorders, when counselling and medicine are combined, and drug use in pregnancy when counselling needs to go beyond the medical treatment to explore the thoughts and feelings of the client about her drug use and the birth. Psychotic episodes, overdoses and suicide attempts are often left to the medical profession to deal with but in each of these there is a vital part of the therapeutic work which only the counsellor can do. It is the job of the counsellor to stay involved with the client and not abandon him.

Prescribed drugs may contribute to antisocial behaviour sometimes and for those who counsel clients about alcohol or illegal drugs, their clients are often using prescribed drugs too. Finally the increasing use of counselling in the workplace means that problems identified there need to include an assessment of the client's drug use. The use of litigation to deal with medical mistakes is not always in the best interests of the client but has become a significant part of the approach to benzodiazepine dependence.

Eating disorders

Eating disorders are similar in many ways to other addictions in that their treatment requires a considerable amount of time being devoted to contemplating change, increasing motivation to change and harm reduction strategies before the addictive behaviour can be worked with. The counselling has to take this into account and recognize that in addition to the use of food or food limitation there may be other behavioural issues that the counsellor must work with in the early stages.

Pressure from others, particularly the family of young sufferers of anorexia, to put on weight or eat regularly can drive a person who feels desperate not to get fat, to use vomiting or laxatives to get rid of the food. Diuretics may be used to reduce body fluid and hence weight, and because the sufferer may hide the condition from family and general practitioner this abuse of drugs may go unrecognized for a while. These methods of control are more dangerous from a medical point of view than starvation itself.

What makes this area complex is that it frequently requires both a medical and a counselling intervention and since they may have different objectives especially over issues such as control, it is difficult to judge which approach is more vital at any stage and when and how they may be combined. If integrated working is possible, for example where the client is an in-patient, it is important that the counsellor does not lose sight of the long-term objective to deal with the underlying psychological issue, while accepting and welcoming the part medicine has to play particularly in harm reduction.

Where treatment is shared, perhaps between general practitioner and counsellor, cooperation and discussion are vital, unless the two stages are going to be kept separate although it is hard to see how they could be. Certainly when the client is alternating between starvation and bingeing and using drugs or vomiting, the risk to the client's health and life must take precedence and the counsellor will not be able to engage the client until there is greater stability.

The part that laxatives and diuretics play in the client's battle for control is described by Duker and Slade (1988) and they also discuss 'bad medicine' and 'good medicine' in ways that help the counsellor to understand the prescribing. Because the eating problem is easily disguised in the early stages, and may be shown in antisocial or inappropriate behaviour, the prescriber may not see the underlying disorder. In the past this may have resulted in the use of appetite stimulants or appetite suppressants. These have generally been replaced by dietary advice.

Chlorpromazine has been widely advocated for use in anorexia nervosa but this is more likely to be in an in-patient setting. Its purpose is to reduce the anxiety the patient feels over re-feeding programmes and is probably less psychologically damaging than forcing the patient to eat. Benzodiazepines may be used for the same purpose but the dependence potential means they are probably restricted to short courses, although some doctors would argue that the benefits in getting the patient to eat outweigh the risks.

Antidepressants have less dependence potential than benzodiazepines, although they are more toxic in overdose, but they may have a useful role to play in providing a holding function for the very depressed client. Benzodiazepines may contribute to depression and suicidal thoughts and feelings, but some of the newer antidepressants, such as fluoxetine which is prescibed at a higher dose of 60mg per day for bulimia, are not without risk to the seriously suicidal client.

Duker and Slade (1988), in a chapter on 'good medicine', give the counsellor some useful guidelines on when medical intervention is necessary or useful. Extreme emaciation, very low body weight and being inaccessible for counselling probably mean a medical referral is necessary and the counsellor should not hesitate to do this, with the prior consent of the client. Motivating, supporting and continuing to listen are still important and the client needs to know that the counsellor is not abandoning her and will continue where possible to promote the client's autonomy.

In hospital, sedation may reduce the client's distress, reduce feelings of panic if staff are not available to talk, or prevent self-harm such as cutting or suicide attempts. Duker and Slade (1988) point out that medication in no way 'cures' the eating problem and that the lowest dose possible should be used only as long as necessary so as not to interfere with psychotherapeutic treatment. This is where the counsellor comes in again and when the counselling relationship provides the necessary stability, the drugs can be gradually discontinued.

Drugs and pregnancy

An authoritative statement about the effects of drugs in pregnancy (Appendix 4, *British National Formulary*) states that:

> Drugs can have harmful effects on the fetus at any time during pregnancy.

> During the first trimester they may produce congenital malformations, and the period of greatest risk is from the third to the eleventh week of pregnancy.

> During the second and third trimester drugs may affect the growth and functional development of the fetus or have toxic effects on fetal tissues; and drugs given shortly before term or during labour may have adverse effects on labour or on the neonate after delivery.

Clients taking psychotropic drugs over a period of time may want to or become pregnant, and be concerned about the implications. Abstinence from psychotropic medication for two weeks before conception is thought to be the only way to reduce to nil the risk to the fetus. However the extent of the risk, both to the baby and therefore the mother, needs to be weighed against the benefits to the mother of taking drugs.

Specific cautions are given in the *British National Formulary* but congenital malformations are unlikely if low doses are used. Counsellors whose clients are using benzodiazepines often in conjunction with other substances in high doses or chaotically would need to get further advice. Mostly, the neonate experiences side-effects of the drug or withdrawal symptoms after birth. The first step would be for the client to inform her general practitioner that she is pregnant so that her drug use can be considered in the antenatal care which is offered.

If the benefit to the client of continuing her drugs outweighs the risks, then the counsellor needs to explore with her fears about harming the baby, guilt about using drugs, or fantasies about what will happen when the child is born. If drugs can be withdrawn, then this may prove to be sufficiently motivating for the client to be willing to reconsider her drug use. If she decides to continue, then accepting the responsibility may bring to the surface past insecurities and conflicts about her own and others' needs.

If drugs are to be withdrawn, it is still more important to withdraw gradually than to reduce the time during which the fetus is exposed to drugs. First, abrupt cessation, or rapid withdrawal of benzodiazepines in particular, increases the likelihood of fits, severe withdrawal symptoms and abortion especially in the first and third trimester. Secondly, rapid withdrawal may put the client under unacceptable psychological pressure and emotional distress, at a time when she may be feeling more emotionally vulnerable.

The counsellor can engage the client who is continuing her drug use or withdrawing during pregnancy in thinking through the implications and preparing for the birth. It may help the client to have questions which she wants to discuss at the antenatal clinic. These could include:

1 Will it have to be a hospital delivery rather than a choice between that and home delivery?
2 Is there any way fears about congenital malformation can be investigated before the birth? Does the client want that?
3 What should the client expect will be different about her baby because of the drug use? Will it be more distressed or less responsive?
4 Will the baby thrive in the same way and what can the client look out for?

5 Might the baby require special care for respiration or feeding? Will that mean being separated?
6 What will be different for the client? Is a normal method of delivery still possible or the most likely?
7 Will the client still have her feelings about the baby? How will the drug use affect the bonding?
8 Is this the first pregnancy and if not, what happened last time? Does the client want anything to be different?
9 Has the client been depressed and does she have worries about being depressed after the birth?
10 What expectations of herself as a mother does the client have and how does that relate to her experience of being mothered?

The implications of taking prescribed drugs and breast-feeding are described in the *British National Formulary* (Appendix 5).

Psychotic episodes

A wide view of these episodes might include hallucinations, delusions, depersonalization, perceptual distortions and a sense of unreality. Other severe reactions such as seizures and fits, extreme levels of depression or manic episodes can be approached by the counsellor in a similar way. There are three main questions the counsellor must ask herself:

1 How serious is it?
2 What is it about?
3 What shall I do about it?

If the answer to the first question is that the client is in crisis, then sometimes emergency referral takes precedence.

The first time the client has an experience of this kind is much more worrying for him, his relatives and friends or his carers. It is the unexpected and unpredictable event which precipitates a crisis. If it has happened before, the expected difficulties can be prepared for which makes containing them much easier. The immediate support which is available to the client should be assessed and in particular that he is not on his own. If a neighbour or relative stranger is informing the counsellor, then the client may be seriously unsupported.

The severity of the incident is affected by whether the client is at risk of harming himself or others and how soon and how easily the situation can be returned to safety again. A further factor may be how accessible the counsellor is to the client. In health care settings, the counsellor may be able to reach the client very quickly; where the client is at home contact may only be possible by telephone. The existing involvement by the client's general practitioner or psychiatric services may mean that others will respond to the seriousness of the event.

Exploring what the psychotic episode is about requires two levels of enquiry: first the events in the present which may have precipitated it and secondly, the underlying or predisposing factors. Since the client is or has been taking drugs, the counsellor can check whether the symptoms are side-effects (*British National Formulary*) or withdrawal effects (Hammersley and Hamlin, 1990; Lacey, 1991). Clearly the context is important such as whether the client has recently stopped, increased or reduced his drugs. It may also be important to ask whether the client has been using any other psychotropic substances such as alcohol, illegal drugs or solvents.

The predisposing factors which the counsellor should investigate such as a previous history of psychosis, paranoia or evidence of dementia, may already be known from the assessment. However since withdrawal of drugs often uncovers more than the client was aware of at the beginning of counselling, there may be memories of early sexual, physical and psychological abuse which now emerge. If much of the client's early life remains inaccessible, the counsellor may recognize the signs which suggest such a history.

Before deciding what action to take, it is advisable for the counsellor to seek a second opinion or to discuss matters with her supervisor or clinical manager. Some counselling settings have this process built into the structures whereas others do not. Working in statutory services may give the counsellor immediate medical or psychiatric support but may have the disadvantage that the decisions and the client are taken out of the counsellor's hands. Working in the private sector may mean that the counsellor has to have strategies set up for immediate supervision and support.

There are two main options open to the counsellor and client: either they can make sense of the episode, decide that it is temporary and agree that it is manageable with the counsellor's support; or they decide that the client does not feel sufficiently safe with this and they need to ask for further help. The decision will be influenced by whether the counsellor can help the client to stay in touch with reality and whether that can be maintained when the counsellor is not present. The context of the family, residential hostel or living alone and how other people respond needs to be taken into account also.

Case example

Penny had been gradually reducing chlordiazepoxide (a benzo-diazepine) over a period of months having previously come off too quickly and had to go back on again. This time she was in control of it herself. She seemed to be extremely sensitive to withdrawal effects so that even tiny reductions produced a massive reaction and one of her doctors said it could not possibly be a withdrawal reaction.

She reduced from 10 mg to 7.5 mg, and a week later when the reaction seemed at a peak she 'saw' trees growing out of the television set towards her and felt terrified and out of control. She telephoned her counsellor who reassured her and her husband that it was a withdrawal reaction and that people did not suddenly go 'off their heads' without a reason.

The counsellor suggested that her family stay with her over the next few days and keep her active and engaged with them and in touch with reality. She stopped watching television for the time being. Penny was reminded that she could ring the counsellor during the day if it happened again, got worse or she needed more support. The psychotic episodes occurred each time she reduced until she was off but she gradually gained control over them.

Case example

Rosemary was withdrawing from both antidepressants and benzo-diazepines and had telephoned the counsellor and had extra sessions because she felt frightened about nightmares which she experienced while she was awake. She found it hard to stay in touch with reality when she was not in contact with the counsellor and she lived alone and was increasingly frightened. Her only relative nearby was her unmarried brother but the nature of her hallucinations and nightmares suggested to the counsellor that he might have been part of the original problem.

When a neighbour telephoned to say that Rosemary had called on her in a 'terrible state', the counsellor asked her to stay with Rosemary while the counsellor telephoned the general practitioner to ask her to make a house call. The GP arranged for an assessment and admission to hospital within a few hours.

The hope was that the drugs could be monitored and adjusted to provide some containment of her severe reaction. In fact the hospital staff had no idea what was happening, assumed she had a psychotic illness and prescribed accordingly. Although the counsellor maintained contact with Rosemary in hospital, no attempt was made to provide integrated care and she spent her time making beds and baskets.

Overdoses and suicide attempts

Clients who are thinking about suicide or want to escape from their painful feelings, if they have been prescribed drugs, have the means. Antipsychotics, antidepressants and lithium are dangerous in overdose and the warning signs are described in the section of the *British National Formulary* which deals with, 'Emergency treatment of poisoning'. Medical help should be sought immediately.

The benzodiazepines are less dangerous in overdose *when taken alone* and this is partly why they so quickly replaced barbiturates. However when taken in combination with alcohol and/or over-the-counter medicines they are dangerous too. In fact many common analgesics are more dangerous than many people are aware of. Counsellors should put the safety of their client first and seek medical help. Understanding the behaviour can come later.

If medical help or hospital admission is needed, the client will then be treated following the medical model at least during the emergency and sometimes beyond. This may mean that the staff act without reference to either the general practitioner or the counsellor. While saving the client's life is a success in itself, some treatment may go beyond that and be helpful to the client in exploring some of the wider issues. Some of what is offered is not so helpful and may include:

1 Stopping drugs abruptly or refusing to re-prescribe.
2 Stopping drugs abruptly and prescribing something else.
3 Ignoring the existing treatment, i.e. counselling, and replacing it with non-treatment, i.e. being 'seen' by a psychiatrist.
4 Being 'told off' and given a stern warning about 'attention-seeking' which is seen as a shameful behaviour.
5 Inadvertently replicating bad childhood experiences, i.e. being over-powered, losing control, being abused, ignoring distress, removing freedom.
6 Encourage splitting by installing two kinds of treatment at the same time, possibly with different objectives.

Smaller overdoses, sometimes called 'trivial', and other acts of self-harm can probably be dealt with by the counsellor if the client's life is not immediately threatened. This may include the client who has suicidal thoughts but does not make serious preparations or attempts. Sometimes the angry feelings against the self are expressed through cutting and self-mutilation, and alcohol binges may serve the same psychological purpose.

What the counsellor needs to do:

1 Establish the facts and encourage the client to share what has been kept hidden.
2 Review what the client was thinking and feeling.
3 Discuss what prompted the attempt/self-harm: a cry for help, seeking attention for what, the precipitating factors.
4 Ask who is being punished, or against whom it is revenge.
5 Explore the implicit message to the counsellor.
6 Consider asking the client to make a contract with the counsellor not to attempt suicide/self-harm but to deal with the feelings in the counselling sessions instead.

The purpose of the no-suicide contract is to give the client safety by removing the conflict between the part of the client who wants to murder and the other part who is in danger; the decision is taken out of the client's hands. This may increase the safety and the client should feel 'held' not punished, by such a contract. Because there is an underlying negative message to the counsellor in self-harm attempts, it is important that the counsellor ensures there is adequate supervision and support for herself.

Disinhibition and antisocial acts

Many people who have been imprisoned or otherwise punished by the criminal justice system suffer from mental illness and psychological problems. There is considerable prescribing within the prison system and while some of this is undoubtedly for reasons of social control, some of it reflects the high incidence of mental illness in the prison population.

Antipsychotic drugs (e.g. chlorpromazine) are prescribed for excitement and violent or dangerously impulsive behaviour as well as for the acute stages of mania. Lithium is used in the 'prophylaxis and treatment' (*British National Formulary*) of mania which might lead to disinhibition or unsocial acts. It also controls aggression or self-mutilating behaviour. Deviant antisocial sexual behaviour is controlled by antipsychotic drugs too. All of these are treatments of the behaviour not the underlying cause.

However disinhibition or antisocial behaviour may result from the prescribing where the level of self-control is lowered and feelings of anger are set free. Alcohol may increase these effects. Although all benzodiazepines are sedatives, some people taking them experience a paradoxical increase in hostility and aggression which ranges from talkativeness and excitement to aggression and antisocial acts. It is usually dose-related and increasing or lowering the dose can make a difference. Benzodiazepines are often prescribed for tension which may be a physical manifestation of suppressed anger.

Antidepressants can make some people more depressed and have the potential to precipitate suicide in severely dysfunctional clients perhaps by lifting the depression sufficiently to enable the person to proceed with the suicidal behaviour. The underlying anger in depression may be felt against others or the self and the depression is a defence against acting on it. Therefore while the prescribing of antidepressants may be helpful when clients are extremely depressed, the counsellor needs to ensure the client's continued safety.

Stealing by clients who have eating disorders as well as taking drugs poses the difficulty of distinguishing what has contributed to what. While the drugs may have had a disinhibiting effect, Duker and Slade (1988) point out that the behaviour may be partly due to the sufferer's biochemically altered state and that this can be used to mount a successful defence because of the lack of prior dishonest intent.

Alcohol

Alcohol is widely known to have disinhibiting effects which is why it is used to facilitate social gatherings. The effects are increased when it is taken with benzodiazepines and some of the consequences may be less desirable. It is used by many people as a relaxant particularly after stressful events. Its sedative effects help people to sleep but its half-life is short and the withdrawal effects can wake people up after a few hours. The interactions between alcohol and prescribed drugs are outlined in Appendix 1 of the *British National Formulary*.

Clients who have a problem with alcohol and have become physically dependent may be prescribed benzodiazepines for their anticonvulsant properties during a detoxification programme. The drugs should not be continued beyond the programme because the client will exchange one dependence for another. However the drugs are controlled by the prescriber, are less easily available than alcohol and cause less liver damage, so they may become part of the maintenance programme for a while.

If the client has a double dependency on prescribed drugs and alcohol, then it is usual to deal with the alcohol problem first, and make quite sure that the client has time to adjust before the prescribed drugs are tackled. If the client does not think he has a problem with alcohol and decides to reduce his prescribed drugs, he should be advised to monitor his drinking to make sure that he is not substituting alcohol for the drugs. Alcohol is no better substitute for real solutions.

Illegal drugs

Dual dependency is a frequent occurrence with clients using illegal drugs and 'topping up' with benzodiazepines when they can get them. They may be obtained on prescription or on the streets. However, by far the most significant prescribing is the maintenance prescribing of methadone, which may later lead to a gradual reduction programme if the client wants to stop using drugs.

Counsellors targeting clients using illegal drugs face similar problems to the counsellor working with clients taking benzo-diazepines in engaging the client. Outreach work has traditionally replaced the wide-ranging advertising that services for prescribed drug users can use to reach and engage the client. The offer of maintenance prescribing of methadone has been very successful in engaging clients, just as arranging with general practitioners to continue to prescribe benzodiazepines for dependent clients has been.

The second step has been to minimize the harm to the client so that he does not commit crimes to finance his drug use, is at less risk due to impurities, multiple use and overdosing, and is encouraged to take drugs orally rather than by injecting to reduce the risks associated with shared needles. During these two stages the client is prepared to contemplate changing his drug use and making life-style changes. Counselling is focused on increasing motivation and developing life-skills.

One of the particular problems associated with working with this client group has been that of getting clients to proceed through all the stages to reduce and come off their drugs and then deal with the underlying issue. It appears that the skills of closely identifying with the client, learning the language and mores of the street culture and knowing about the drugs, which are so useful in engaging the client and helping him survive, get in the way of establishing a therapeutic counselling relationship.

When the client is ready to engage in a therapeutic counselling relationship, such closeness can easily slide into over-identification with the client and the counsellor can struggle to maintain boundaries and differences. It is not the responsibility of the client to deal with this problem. Perhaps it is not the fault of the counsellor either and it needs to be recognized that the two styles of working cannot be offered by the counsellor to *the same client*.

Instead the client is referred on to another counsellor who can establish a different relationship.

Whereas a counsellor working with clients taking prescribed drugs may work at all the stages of engaging, stabilizing, reducing, life-skills development and therapeutic counselling, counsellors working with clients taking illegal drugs often cannot. Perhaps they need to recognize that this client group needs two counsellors: one to engage them, minimize harm and teach life-skills, and one who may teach life-skills; and deal with underlying therapeutic issues.

Not being able to offer all the client needs does not mean that drug counsellors have to specialize or that there is an inherent hierarchy which puts therapeutic counselling at the more advanced end and engagement at the beginner's end. It may mean that the counsellor offers different stages of the counselling process to different clients and does not attempt to work with one client all the way through, when the two approaches seem to be incompatible.

Drugs and the workplace

Counsellors who are aware that prescribed drugs affect thinking, feeling and behaviour have a duty to consider the implications of that for the client in his workplace as much as the doctor does. In some ways the counsellor is better placed than the doctor to do so because the context of the client's life comes up in counselling in more detail than it may do in a medical consultation.

Nearly everybody has a workplace in one sense or another, whether they are employed or do voluntary work, indoors or outdoors, at home or at college; and even if the person is retired from paid work, they may still work in a kitchen, garden or car. Prescribed drugs affect a person's performance and this is particularly important if the client drives or operates machinery or does work involving fine motor coordination or visual-spatial ability. Clients need to be aware of this. Of course the effects of the drugs may be desired ones, such as when beta-blockers are used to control trembling hands when people are anxious.

For counsellors whose work is entirely in the workplace, it is usual to be working in brief focused interventions. Assessment is crucial in this case to determine whether the problem needs short- or long-term help, and so assessing the drug use should play a part in every assessment. There are four questions:

1 Does the drug use exclude short-term counselling? Does it indicate how far back the problem goes?

2   In determining the focus, will the drug issue have to be dealt with first?
3   Can one problem be dealt with, leaving the drug issue until later or leaving it alone?
4   Does this client need to be referred on immediately?

There are some issues and areas where drugs may be contributing to or affecting the problem in some way. Some examples of under-commitment are:

- poor motivation
- working below capacity
- failure to make progress or achieve promotion
- inability to relate to others
- lateness or frequent absences
- failure to implement training or instruction.

Some examples of overcommitment are:

- overworking
- failure to take prescribed rest periods or holidays
- unrealistic expectations of self, others or the organization
- burn-out
- conflict with others.

Drugs may contribute to or affect:

- work-related anxiety
- depression
- personality problems
- difficulty with authority
- interpersonal relationships
- shyness.
- creativity for artists, musicians, actors and writers
- performance for sportsmen and sportswomen, actors, musicians
- examination stress and anxiety for students
- depression/feelings of loss after performance or on completion of creative work; for example, book, painting, composition, play.

Litigation

Clients who are involved in litigation with drug companies, hospitals or their general practitioners pose a particular difficulty for the counsellor because their lives, problems and symptoms are for the period litigation is proceeding 'on hold'. It is as if everything has become 'frozen' while the court action becomes the main priority rather than their counselling. The anger which the client feels is withdrawn from a desire to overcome his problems and is invested elsewhere.

The group action which was started against the manufacturers of benzodiazepines has been unsuccessful so far, leaving many people with additional disappointments to face. There have been successful cases of complaints against doctors and hospitals for negligence, but many clients do not always appreciate that what may appear perfectly obvious to them, has to be proved to the satisfaction of the court.

Since many of the cases depend on proving that the client has suffered damage as a result of the prescribing, it is important to realize that damage will probably be assessed by psychiatrists who will see things from a medical perspective not a psychological one. It is likely that both the medical and legal professions do not recognize the difference officially. Evidence that a 'psychiatric condition' existed before the drugs were prescribed will be taken to show that the drugs cannot be proved to be the cause of the damage, and that the condition might have worsened anyway without the treatment.

What is right or wrong and just or unjust may not come into it and the hoped for solution of an admission of a mistake and an apology may not materialize. There may have been some validity in the client's complaint – there often is – but it is unlikely to be therapeutically helpful for the client to try again, by joining in group protests, victim schemes and petitions. It may be more helpful to direct the client to see his part in it, his responsibility for accepting the diagnosis and prescriptions. It may be a very painful lesson for the client to discover he was too trusting.

Some implications for counselling:

1 The client may 'hang on' to symptoms which are needed to prove he has been harmed, waiting for the case to be resolved.
2 The failure of the case in court may mean the client will not give up the case and therefore the symptoms, and move on.
3 Anger is directed at others and the client's responsibility is denied or minimized.
4 The focus on litigation may take most of the client's attention.
5 The client is focused on some future event which will provide a 'cure', and may not want to look backwards for the origins of the problem.
6 The counsellor may have a lot to undo before she gets to the start of the problem proper.

7 The counsellor may have difficulty validating the client's feelings about a chapter of medical mistakes without colluding with the client's desire to put all the blame on the doctor or the drugs.
8 The prescriber may have become defensive and over-cautious and be unwilling to continue to prescribe when it is necessary.
9 The prescriber may punish and reject the client who then becomes labelled a 'difficult patient'.
10 The relationship between the prescriber and the counsellor may be adversely affected if the counsellor is drawn in to take sides.

Maintaining professional equality

Medicine and counselling are separate professions each with a knowledge base, skills, ethics, ways of working, training and qualifications, remuneration and status. They have different traditions, assumptions, languages and hierarchies. They have different models of emotional distress. There is a need for separateness so that counsellors do not adopt the medical model and this is much easier to do from outside when the counsellor is not employed by the doctor.

The treatment of psychological problems and drugs is a 'grey area' because the two professions overlap, and it is unclear who has the expertise in what. It is tempting for the counsellor to assume that doctors know all about drugs and for doctors to assume counsellors know nothing. It is equally tempting for counsellors to assume they know all about psychological problems and doctors know nothing. The difficulty is further compounded by whose responsibility the patient is: the doctor may assume the patient is his, the counsellor may assume the client is responsible for himself.

This 'grey area' does not exist in a vacuum but in a social context that gives a lot of power to the medical profession. It is culturally accepted that doctors are not to be challenged, by the patient, by his family and by the counsellor. That has and is changing and many people in both professions welcome that. However counsellors may have to work quite hard not to adopt a one-down position in relation to doctors and give away too much power by over-explaining themselves.

Maintaining professional equality is helped by recognizing that the two professions do not always speak the same language even when they use the same words and that each has to learn something of the other's language. Each profession has something to offer the other and it is not just the client or patient who benefits. When the counsellor and doctor establish a relationship based on mutual respect, they may both gain from it.

Conclusion

All counsellors will at some time encounter clients who are taking prescribed drugs and the drugs affect the counselling. Sometimes the drugs are helpful, frequently they are not. There are specialist counsellors whose work is primarily with clients who have drug problems but most counsellors will be non-specialists who want a sense that they can tackle the drug issue confidently when it arises. This book has sought to give counsellors from a variety of backgrounds a broad view of the subject.

First, it has tackled the theoretical problem that the medical and psychological models of emotional distress are different. That means that in future discussions with doctors, counsellors will be able to make their case from a sound theoretical base. Knowledge of psychotropic drugs, their uses and limitations, gives the counsellor the facts to support her argument. It also starts the process of redefining treatment objectives in wider terms than the management of symptoms.

Secondly, it has tackled the issue of how to integrate drugs into the assessment of clients so that the implications are taken into account in the counselling process. No one model of counselling is needed but the case is made for flexibility and innovation. A structured approach to what may be a very long process helps the counsellor to orientate herself at each stage and keep a sense of movement and progress. Where things have not gone as expected in counselling, this may help the counsellor identify what was wrong or where expectations were unrealistic.

Finally the most important aspect that this book challenges is the hierarchical view that puts medicine at the top and sees counselling as 'something which may be useful'. Counselling as the treatment of choice is what many patients have looked for and longed for when they have taken their problems to their general practitioner. Too often the problem has been medicalized, managed and made worse. Counsellors have competences which can be liberated by a change in their attitude to medicine from passive acceptance to informed challenge.

References

British Association for Counselling (1989) *Invitation to Membership*. Rugby: BAC.

British Medical Association and The Royal Pharmaceutical Society (1994) *British National Formulary*. London: The Pharmaceutical Press (published six monthly).

Committee on the Review of Medicines (1980) 'Systematic review of the benzodiazepines', *British Medical Journal*, 280: 910–12.

Dilsaver, S.C (1989) 'Antidepressant withdrawal syndromes: phenomenology and pathophysiology', *Acta Psychiatrica Scandinavica*, 79: 113–17.

Draucker, C.B. (1992) *Counselling Survivors of Childhood Sexual Abuse*. London: Sage.

Duker, M. and Slade, R. (1988) *Anorexia Nervosa and Bulimia: How to Help*. Milton Keynes: Open University Press.

Finkelhor, D. and Browne, A. (1985) 'The traumatic impact of child sexual abuse: a conceptualization', *American Journal of Orthopsychiatry*, 55: 530–41.

Fontana, D. (1990) *Social Skills at Work*. London: British Psychological Society/Routledge.

Hammersley, D.E. and Hamlin, M.A. (1990) *The Benzodiazepine Manual: A Professional Guide to Withdrawal*. Wedmore: Healthskills.

Holmes, J. (1993) *John Bowlby and Attachment Theory*. London: Routledge.

International Drug Therapy News (1984) 'Antidepressant withdrawal reactions', 19: 23–4.

Johnstone, L. (1989) *Users and Abusers of Psychiatry*. London: Routledge.

Lacey, R. (1991) *The Complete Guide to Psychiatric Drugs: a Layman's Handbook*. London: MIND/Ebury Press.

Lader, M. et al. (1992) 'Guidelines for the management of patients with generalised anxiety: consensus statement', *Psychiatric Bulletin*, 16: 560–5.

Paykel, E.S. and Priest, R.G. (1992) 'Recognition and management of depression in general practice: consensus statement', *British Medical Journal*, 305: 1198–202.

Pitman, E. (1991) *This Won't Change your Life (but it Might Help)*. Clevedon: Channel View Books.

Rowe, D. (1991) *The Depression Handbook*. London: Collins.

Stewart, I. and Joines, V. (1987) *TA Today: a New Introduction to Transactional Analysis*. Nottingham: Lifespace.

Ware, P. (1983) 'Personality adaptations (doors to therapy)', *Transactional Analysis Journal*, 13: 11–19.

Worden, J.W. (1982) *Grief Counselling and Grief Therapy*. London: Tavistock.

Index